BIG IDEAS MATH®
Modeling Real Life

Grade 1
Volume 2

Ron Larson
Laurie Boswell

Big Ideas Learning™

Erie, Pennsylvania
BigIdeasLearning.com

Big Ideas Learning, LLC
1762 Norcross Road
Erie, PA 16510-3838
USA

For product information and customer support, contact Big Ideas Learning at **1-877-552-7766** or visit us at ***BigIdeasLearning.com***.

Cover Image:
Valdis Torms, bgblue/DigitalVision Vectors/Getty Images

Copyright © 2022 by Big Ideas Learning, LLC. All rights reserved.

No part of this work may be reproduced or transmitted in any form or by any means, electronic or mechanical, including, but not limited to, photocopying and recording, or by any information storage or retrieval system, without prior written permission of Big Ideas Learning, LLC, unless such copying is expressly permitted by copyright law. Address inquiries to Permissions, Big Ideas Learning, LLC, 1762 Norcross Road, Erie, PA 16510.

Big Ideas Learning and *Big Ideas Math* are registered trademarks of Larson Texts, Inc.

Printed in the U.S.A.

ISBN 13: 978-1-64727-928-8

2 3 4 5 6 7 8 9 10—25 24 23 22 21

One Voice from Kindergarten Through Algebra 2

Written by renowned authors, Dr. Ron Larson and Dr. Laurie Boswell, *Big Ideas Math* offers a seamless math pedagogy from elementary through high school. Together, Ron and Laurie provide a consistent voice that encourages students to make connections through cohesive progressions and clear instruction. Since 1992, Ron and Laurie have authored over 50 mathematics programs.

> *Each time Laurie and I start working on a new program, we spend time putting ourselves in the position of the reader. How old is the reader? What is the reader's experience with mathematics? The answers to these questions become our writing guides. Our goal is to make the learning targets understandable and to develop these targets in a clear path that leads to student success.*
>
> — Ron Larson

Ron Larson, Ph.D., is well known as lead author of a comprehensive and widely used mathematics program that ranges from elementary school through college. He holds the distinction of Professor Emeritus from Penn State Erie, The Behrend College, where he taught for nearly 40 years. He received his Ph.D. in mathematics from the University of Colorado. Dr. Larson engages in the latest research and advancements in mathematics education and consistently incorporates key pedagogical elements to ensure focus, coherence, rigor, and student self-reflection.

> *My passion and goal in writing is to provide an essential resource for exploring and making sense of mathematics. Our program is guided by research around the learning and teaching of mathematics in the hopes of improving the achievement of all students. May this be a successful year for you!*
>
> — Laurie Boswell

Laurie Boswell, Ed.D., is the former Head of School at Riverside School in Lyndonville, Vermont. In addition to authoring textbooks, she provides mathematics consulting and embedded coaching sessions. Dr. Boswell received her Ed.D. from the University of Vermont in 2010. She is a recipient of the Presidential Award for Excellence in Mathematics Teaching and later served as president of CPAM. Laurie has taught math to students at all levels, elementary through college. In addition, Laurie has served on the NCTM Board of Directors and as a Regional Director for NCSM. Along with Ron, Laurie has co-authored numerous math programs and has become a popular national speaker.

Contributors, Reviewers, and Research

Big Ideas Learning would like to express our gratitude to the mathematics education and instruction experts who served as our advisory panel, contributing specialists, and reviewers during the writing of *Big Ideas Math: Modeling Real Life*. Their input was an invaluable asset during the development of this program.

Contributing Specialists and Reviewers

- **Sophie Murphy**, Ph.D. Candidate, Melbourne School of Education, Melbourne, Australia
  Learning Targets and Success Criteria Specialist and Visible Learning Reviewer
- **Linda Hall**, Mathematics Educational Consultant, Edmond, OK
  Advisory Panel
- **Michael McDowell**, Ed.D., Superintendent, Ross, CA
  Project-Based Learning Specialist
- **Kelly Byrne**, Math Supervisor and Coordinator of Data Analysis, Downingtown, PA
  Advisory Panel
- **Jean Carwin**, Math Specialist/TOSA, Snohomish, WA
  Advisory Panel
- **Nancy Siddens**, Independent Language Teaching Consultant, Las Cruces, NM
  English Language Learner Specialist
- **Kristen Karbon**, Curriculum and Assessment Coordinator, Troy, MI
  Advisory Panel
- **Kery Obradovich**, K–8 Math/Science Coordinator, Northbrook, IL
  Advisory Panel
- **Jennifer Rollins**, Math Curriculum Content Specialist, Golden, CO
  Advisory Panel
- **Becky Walker**, Ph.D., School Improvement Services Director, Green Bay, WI
  Advisory Panel and Content Reviewer
- **Deborah Donovan**, Mathematics Consultant, Lexington, SC
  Content Reviewer
- **Tom Muchlinski**, Ph.D., Mathematics Consultant, Plymouth, MN
  Content Reviewer and Teaching Edition Contributor
- **Mary Goetz**, Elementary School Teacher, Troy, MI
  Content Reviewer
- **Nanci N. Smith**, Ph.D., International Curriculum and Instruction Consultant, Peoria, AZ
  Teaching Edition Contributor
- **Robyn Seifert-Decker**, Mathematics Consultant, Grand Haven, MI
  Teaching Edition Contributor
- **Bonnie Spence**, Mathematics Education Specialist, Missoula, MT
  Teaching Edition Contributor
- **Suzy Gagnon**, Adjunct Instructor, University of New Hampshire, Portsmouth, NH
  Teaching Edition Contributor
- **Art Johnson**, Ed.D., Professor of Mathematics Education, Warwick, RI
  Teaching Edition Contributor
- **Anthony Smith**, Ph.D., Associate Professor, Associate Dean, University of Washington Bothell, Seattle, WA
  Reading and Writing Reviewer
- **Brianna Raygor**, Music Teacher, Fridley, MN
  Music Reviewer
- **Nicole Dimich Vagle**, Educator, Author, and Consultant, Hopkins, MN
  Assessment Reviewer
- **Janet Graham**, District Math Specialist, Manassas, VA
  Response to Intervention and Differentiated Instruction Reviewer
- **Sharon Huber**, Director of Elementary Mathematics, Chesapeake, VA
  Universal Design for Learning Reviewer

Student Reviewers

- T.J. Morin
- Alayna Morin
- Ethan Bauer
- Emery Bauer
- Emma Gaeta
- Ryan Gaeta
- Benjamin SanFrotello
- Bailey SanFrotello
- Samantha Grygier
- Robert Grygier IV
- Jacob Grygier
- Jessica Urso
- Ike Patton
- Jake Lobaugh
- Adam Fried
- Caroline Naser
- Charlotte Naser

Research

Ron Larson and Laurie Boswell used the latest in educational research, along with the body of knowledge collected from expert mathematics instructors, to develop the *Modeling Real Life* series. The pedagogical approach used in this program follows the best practices outlined in the most prominent and widely accepted educational research, including:

- *Visible Learning*, John Hattie © 2009
- *Visible Learning for Teachers*
  John Hattie © 2012
- *Visible Learning for Mathematics*
  John Hattie © 2017
- *Principles to Actions: Ensuring Mathematical Success for All*
  NCTM © 2014
- *Adding It Up: Helping Children Learn Mathematics*
  National Research Council © 2001
- *Mathematical Mindsets: Unleashing Students' Potential through Creative Math, Inspiring Messages and Innovative Teaching*
  Jo Boaler © 2015
- *What Works in Schools: Translating Research into Action*
  Robert Marzano © 2003
- *Classroom Instruction That Works: Research-Based Strategies for Increasing Student Achievement*
  Marzano, Pickering, and Pollock © 2001
- *Principles and Standards for School Mathematics*
  NCTM © 2000
- *Rigorous PBL by Design: Three Shifts for Developing Confident and Competent Learners*
  Michael McDowell © 2017
- *Universal Design for Learning Guidelines*
  CAST © 2011
- *Rigor/Relevance Framework®*
  International Center for Leadership in Education
- *Understanding by Design*
  Grant Wiggins and Jay McTighe © 2005
- Achieve, ACT, and The College Board
- *Elementary and Middle School Mathematics: Teaching Developmentally*
  John A. Van de Walle and Karen S. Karp © 2015
- *Evaluating the Quality of Learning: The SOLO Taxonomy*
  John B. Biggs & Kevin F. Collis © 1982
- *Unlocking Formative Assessment: Practical Strategies for Enhancing Students' Learning in the Primary and Intermediate Classroom*
  Shirley Clarke, Helen Timperley, and John Hattie © 2004
- *Formative Assessment in the Secondary Classroom*
  Shirley Clarke © 2005
- *Improving Student Achievement: A Practical Guide to Assessment for Learning*
  Toni Glasson © 2009

Focus and Coherence from

Instructional Design

A single authorship team from Kindergarten through Algebra 2 results in a logical progression of focused topics with meaningful coherence from course to course.

FOCUS

A focused program dedicates lessons, activities, and assessments to grade-level standards while simultaneously supporting and engaging you in the major work of the course.

The **Learning Target** in your book and the **Success Criteria** in the Teaching Edition focus the learning for each lesson into manageable chunks, with clear teaching text and examples.

Learning Target: Write related addition and subtraction equations to complete a fact family.

Laurie's Notes

Preparing to Teach

Students have heard about time and the language of time. Most students do not understand time or know how to tell time on an analog clock. In this lesson, students are introduced to telling time to the hour. They learn about the hour hand and telling time as o'clock.

Laurie's Notes, located in the Teaching Edition, prepare your teacher for the math concepts in each chapter and lesson and make connections to the threads of major topics for the course.

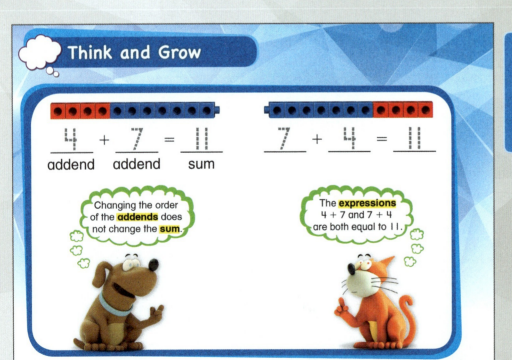

a Single Authorship Team

COHERENCE

A single authorship team built a coherent program that has intentional progression of content within each grade and between grade levels. You will build new understanding on foundations from prior grades and connect concepts throughout the course.

The authors developed content that progresses from prior chapters and grades to future ones. In addition to charts like this one, Laurie's Notes gives your teacher insights about where you have come from and where you are going in your learning progression.

Through the Grades

Kindergarten	Grade 1	Grade 2
• Represent addition and subtraction with various models and strategies. • Solve addition and subtraction word problems within 10. • Fluently add and subtract within 5.	• Solve addition and subtraction word problems within 20. • Fluently add and subtract within 10. • Determine the unknown number to complete addition and subtraction equations.	• Solve addition and subtraction word problems within 100. • Solve word problems involving length and money. • Solve one- and two-step word problems. • Fluently add and subtract within 20.

One author team thoughtfully wrote each course, creating a seamless progression of content from Kindergarten to Algebra 2.

	Grade K	Grade 1	Grade 2	Grade 3	Grade 4	Grade 5	Grade 6	
Number and Quantity	**Number and Operations – Base Ten**				**Number and Operations – Base Ten**		**The Number System**	
	Work with numbers 11–19 to gain foundations for place value. *Chapter 8*	Extend the counting sequence. Use place value and properties of operations to add and subtract. *Chapters 6–9*	Use place value and properties of operations to add and subtract. *Chapters 2–10, 14*	Use place value and properties of operations to perform multi-digit arithmetic. *Chapters 7–9, 12*	Generalize place value understanding for multi-digit whole numbers. Use place value and properties of operations to perform multi-digit arithmetic. *Chapters 1–5*	Understand the place value system. Perform operations with multi-digit whole numbers and with decimals to hundredths. *Chapters 1, 3–7*	Perform operations with multi-digit numbers and find common factors and multiples. *Chapter 1* Divide fractions by fractions. *Chapter 2* Extend understanding of numbers to the rational number system. *Chapter 8*	Perfor rationa Chapte
				Num. and Oper. – Fractions	**Number and Operations – Fractions**		**Ratios and Proportional Relations**	
				Understand fractions as numbers. *Chapters 10, 11, 14*	Extend understanding of fraction equivalence and ordering. Build fractions from unit fractions.	Add, subtract, multiply, and divide fractions. *Chapters 6, 8–11*	Use ratios to solve problems. *Chapters 3, 4*	Use pr to solv Chapte

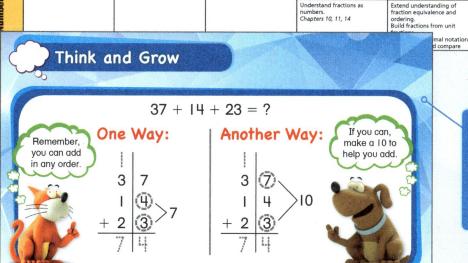

Throughout each course, lessons build on prior learning as new concepts are introduced. Here you are reminded of rules and strategies that you already know to help solve the addition problem.

vii

Rigor in Math: A Balanced Approach

Instructional Design

The authors wrote each chapter and every lesson to provide a meaningful balance of rigorous instruction.

RIGOR
A rigorous program provides a balance of three important building blocks.
- **Conceptual Understanding** Discovering why
- **Procedural Fluency** Learning how
- **Application** Knowing when to apply

Conceptual Understanding
You have the opportunity to develop foundational concepts central to the *Learning Target* in each *Explore and Grow* by experimenting with new concepts, talking with peers, and asking questions.

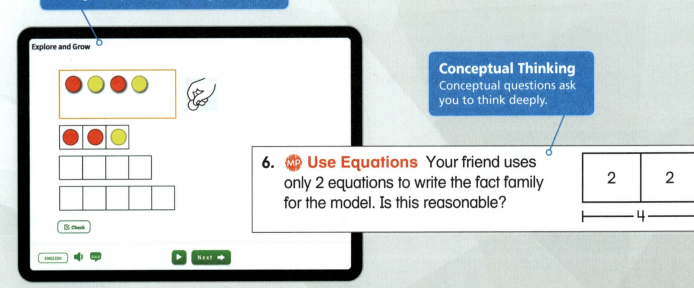

Conceptual Thinking
Conceptual questions ask you to think deeply.

6. **Use Equations** Your friend uses only 2 equations to write the fact family for the model. Is this reasonable?

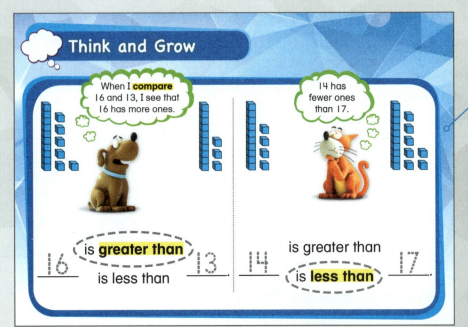

Procedural Fluency
Solidify learning with clear, stepped-out teaching in *Think and Grow* examples.

Then shift conceptual understanding into procedural fluency with *Show and Grow, Apply and Grow, Practice,* and *Review & Refresh.*

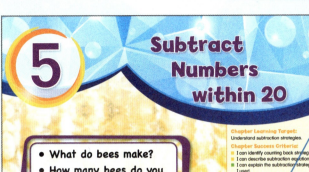

Connecting to Real Life
Begin every chapter thinking about the world around you. Then apply what you learn in the chapter with a related *Performance Task*.

Daily Application Practice
Modeling Real Life, *Dig Deeper*, and other non-routine problems help you apply surface-level skills to gain a deeper understanding. These problems lead to independent problem-solving.

15. **Modeling Real Life** Your magic book has 163 tricks. Your friend's magic book has 100 more tricks than yours. How many tricks does your friend's magic book have?

_____ tricks

16. **DIG DEEPER!** You have 624 songs. Newton has 100 fewer than you. Descartes has 10 more than Newton. How many songs does Descartes have?

_____ songs

THE PROBLEM-SOLVING PLAN

1. **Understand the Problem**
Think about what the problem is asking. Circle what you know and underline what you need to find.

2. **Make a Plan**
Plan your solution pathway before jumping in to solve. Identify any relationships and decide on a problem-solving strategy.

3. **Solve and Check**
As you solve the problem, be sure to evaluate your progress and check your answers. Throughout the problem-solving process, you must continually ask, "Does this make sense?" and be willing to change course if necessary.

Problem-Solving Plan
Walk through the Problem-Solving Plan, featured in many *Think and Grow* examples, to help you make sense of problems with confidence.

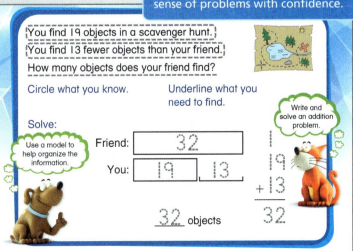

ix

Embedded Mathematical Practices

Encouraging Mathematical Mindsets

Developing proficiency in the **Mathematical Practices** is about becoming a mathematical thinker. Learn to ask why, and reason and communicate with others as you learn. Use this guide to develop proficiency with the mathematical practices.

1 One way to **Make Sense of Problems and Persevere in Solving Them** is to use the Problem-Solving Plan. Take time to analyze the given information and what the problem is asking to help you plan a solution pathway.

Look for labels such as:
- Find Entry Points
- Analyze a Problem
- Interpret a Solution
- Make a Plan
- Use a Similar Problem
- Check Your Work

There are 33 students on a bus. 10 more get on. How many students are on the bus now?

Addition equation:

_____ students

Check Your Work When adding 10, should the digit in the tens place or the ones place change?

5. **Analyze a Problem** Use the numbers shown to write two addition equations.

8 10 2

___ + ___ = ___
___ + ___ = ___

7. **Reasoning** The minute hand points to the 7. What number will it point to in 10 minutes?

2 **Reason Abstractly** when you explore an example using numbers and models to represent the problem. Other times, **Reason Quantitatively** when you see relationships in numbers or models and draw conclusions about the problem.

Look for labels such as:
- Reasoning
- Number Sense
- Use Equations
- Use Expressions

3. **Number Sense** Which numbers can you subtract from 55 without regrouping?

15   49   33   24

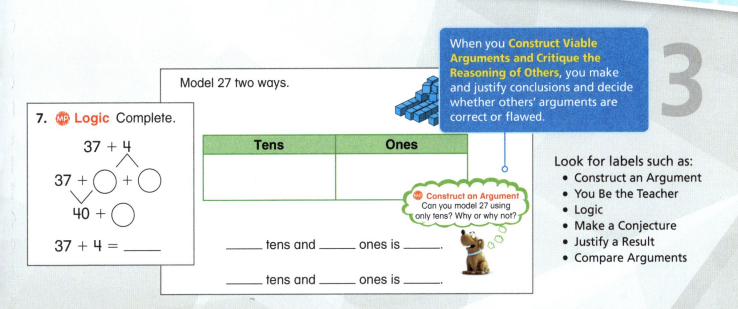

3

When you **Construct Viable Arguments and Critique the Reasoning of Others**, you make and justify conclusions and decide whether others' arguments are correct or flawed.

Look for labels such as:
- Construct an Argument
- You Be the Teacher
- Logic
- Make a Conjecture
- Justify a Result
- Compare Arguments

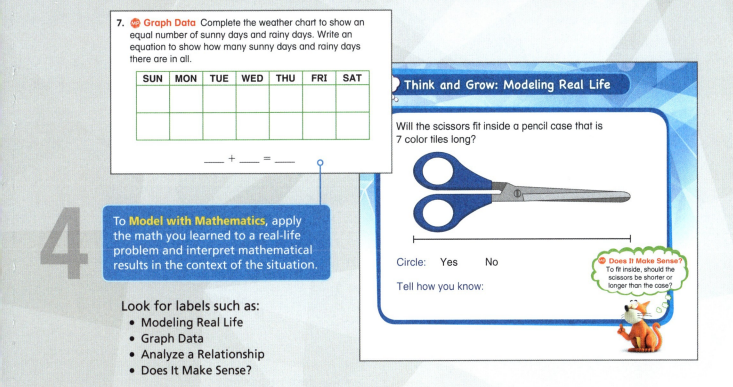

4

To **Model with Mathematics**, apply the math you learned to a real-life problem and interpret mathematical results in the context of the situation.

Look for labels such as:
- Modeling Real Life
- Graph Data
- Analyze a Relationship
- Does It Make Sense?

BUILDING TO FULL UNDERSTANDING

Throughout each course, you have opportunities to demonstrate specific aspects of the mathematical practices. Labels throughout the book indicate gateways to those aspects. Collectively, these opportunities will lead to a full understanding of each mathematical practice. Developing these mindsets and habits will give meaning to the mathematics you learn.

Embedded Mathematical Practices (continued)

5 To **Use Appropriate Tools Strategically**, you need to know what tools are available and think about how each tool might help you solve a mathematical problem. When you choose a tool to use, remember that it may have limitations.

Look for labels such as:
- Choose Tools
- Use Math Tools
- Use Technology

8. **Choose Tools** Would you measure the length of a bus with a centimeter ruler or a meter stick? Why?

Use Math Tools How can you use a drawing to help organize the information given?

11. **DIG DEEPER!** There are 63 people in a theater, 21 people in the lobby, and 10 people in the parking lot. How many more people are in the theater than in both the lobby and the parking lot?

_____ more people

6 When you **Attend to Precision**, you are developing a habit of being careful in how you talk about concepts, label work, and write answers.

Look for labels such as:
- Precision
- Communicate Clearly
- Maintain Accuracy

7. **DIG DEEPER!** Complete the model and the equation to match.

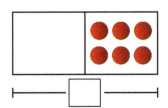

___ + ___ = 8

Communicate Clearly In the model, what shows the addends? the sum?

5. **Precision** Which picture shows the correct way to measure the straw?

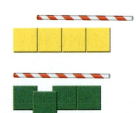

6. **Patterns** Find the sums. Think: What do you notice?

   4 + 5 = ___

   4 + 4 = ___

   5 + 5 = ___

Tens	Ones
☐	
3	8
+ 2	4

   38 + 24 = _____

   Structure What step did you use to find 38 + 24 that you would not use to find 31 + 24? Why?

   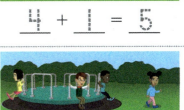

   Look for labels such as:
   • Structure
   • Patterns

7 **Look For and Make Use of Structure** by looking closely to see structure within a mathematical statement, or stepping back for an overview to see how individual parts make one single object.

8. **Repeated Reasoning** What other shape has the same number of surfaces, vertices, and edges as a rectangular prism? How is that shape different from a rectangular prism?

   Find a Rule When you add or subtract 1, what is true about the sum or difference?

   4 + 1 = 5

   4 − 1 = 3

8 When you **Look For and Express Regularity in Repeated Reasoning**, you can notice patterns and make generalizations. Remember to keep in mind the goal of a problem, which will help you evaluate reasonableness of answers along the way.

Look for labels such as:
• Repeated Reasoning
• Find a Rule

Visible Learning Through Learning Targets,

Making Learning Visible

Knowing the learning intention of a chapter or lesson helps you focus on the purpose of an activity, rather than simply completing it in isolation. This program supports visible learning through the consistent use of Learning Targets and Success Criteria to help you become successful.

Every chapter shows a **Learning Target** and four related **Success Criteria**. These are incorporated throughout the chapter content to help guide you in your learning.

Every lesson shows a **Learning Target** that is purposefully integrated into each carefully written lesson.

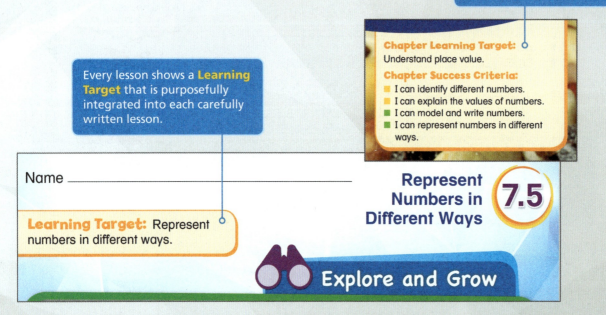

Access the **Learning Target** and **Success Criteria** on every page of the Dynamic Student Edition.

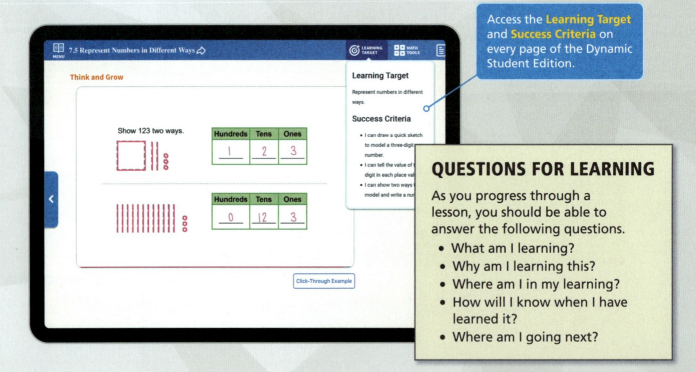

QUESTIONS FOR LEARNING

As you progress through a lesson, you should be able to answer the following questions.

- What am I learning?
- Why am I learning this?
- Where am I in my learning?
- How will I know when I have learned it?
- Where am I going next?

Success Criteria, and Self-Assessment

⊙ Have students indicate with their thumb signals how well they can find the sum in a word problem and write an addition equation. Have students turn and talk with a partner to explain all of the math vocabulary in an addition equation.

Use your thumb signals to rate your understanding of each success criterion. Your teacher will prompt you to self-assess throughout each lesson, and you can keep track of your learning online.

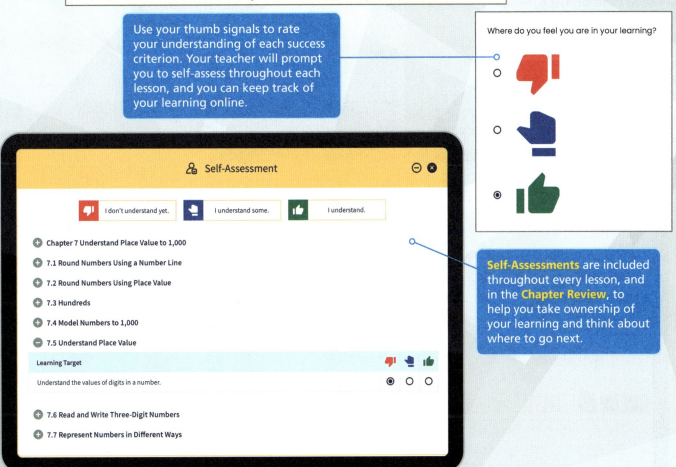

Self-Assessments are included throughout every lesson, and in the **Chapter Review**, to help you take ownership of your learning and think about where to go next.

Ensuring Positive Outcomes

John Hattie's *Visible Learning* research consistently shows that using Learning Targets and Success Criteria can result in two years' growth in one year, ensuring positive outcomes for your learning and achievement.

Sophie Murphy, M.Ed., wrote the chapter-level Learning Targets and Success Criteria for this program. Sophie is currently completing her Ph.D. at the University of Melbourne in Australia with Professor John Hattie as her leading supervisor. Sophie completed her Master's thesis with Professor John Hattie in 2015. Sophie has over 20 years of experience as a teacher and school leader in private and public school settings in Australia.

XV

Strategic Support for Online Learning

Get the Support You Need, When You Need It

There will be times throughout this course when you may need help. Whether you missed a lesson, did not understand the content, or just want to review, take advantage of the resources provided in the *Dynamic Student Edition*.

Use the **Self-Assessment** tool to keep track of your understanding of the lesson's Learning Target and Success Criteria.

Choose **Math Tools** to engage with pattern blocks, digital number lines, linking cubes, and other tools to explore and understand math concepts.

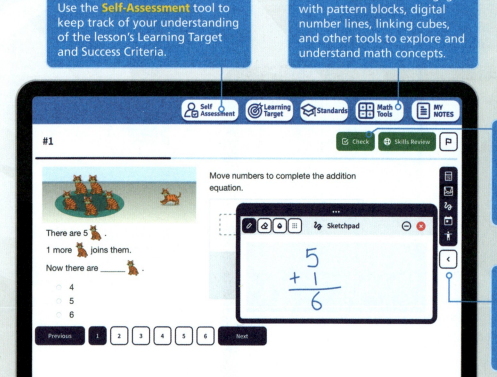

Check your answers to selected exercises as you work through the lesson. Use the **Help** option to view the Digital Example videos.

Use the available **tools**, such as the calculator or sketchpad, to help clearly show your work and demonstrate your math knowledge.

USE THESE QR CODES TO EXPLORE ADDITIONAL RESOURCES

Multi-Language Glossary
View definitions and examples of vocabulary words

Skills Trainer
Practice previously learned skills

Interactive Tools
Visualize mathematical concepts

Skills Review Handbook
A collection of review topics

Learning with Newton and Descartes

Who are Newton and Descartes?

Newton and Descartes are helpful math assistants who appear throughout your math book! They encourage you to think deeply about concepts and develop strong mathematical mindsets with Mathematical Practice questions.

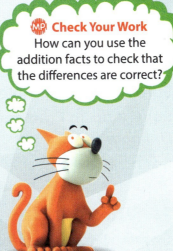

MP Check Your Work
How can you use the addition facts to check that the differences are correct?

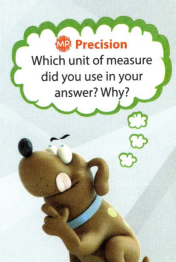

MP Precision
Which unit of measure did you use in your answer? Why?

Newton & Descartes's Math Musicals

Math Musicals offer an engaging connection between math, literature, and music! Newton and Descartes team up in these educational stories and songs to bring mathematics to life!

Math Musicals animation and story

Sheet Music

Addition and Subtraction Situations

Vocabulary 2
- 1.1 Addition: *Add To* 3
- 1.2 Solve *Add To* Problems 9
- 1.3 Solve *Put Together* Problems 15
- 1.4 Solve *Put Together* Problems with Both Addends Unknown 21
- 1.5 Solve *Take From* Problems 27
- 1.6 Solve *Compare* Problems: More 33
- 1.7 Solve *Compare* Problems: Fewer 39
- 1.8 Solve *Add To* Problems with Change Unknown 45
- 1.9 Connect *Put Together* and *Take Apart* Problems 51

Performance Task: Birds 57
Game: Three in a Row 58
Chapter Practice 59

Fluency and Strategies within 10

Vocabulary 64
- 2.1 Add 0 65
- 2.2 Subtract 0 and Subtract All 71
- 2.3 Add and Subtract 1 77
- 2.4 Add Doubles from 1 to 5 83
- 2.5 Use Doubles 89
- 2.6 Add in Any Order 95
- 2.7 Count On to Add 101
- 2.8 Count Back to Subtract 107
- 2.9 Use Addition to Subtract 113

Performance Task: Flowers 119
Game: Add or Subtract 120
Chapter Practice 121

■ Major Topic
■ Supporting Topic
■ Additional Topic

3 More Addition and Subtraction Situations

Vocabulary 126

- 3.1 Solve *Add To* Problems with Start Unknown 127
- 3.2 Solve *Take From* Problems with Change Unknown 133
- 3.3 Solve *Take From* Problems with Start Unknown 139
- 3.4 *Compare* Problems: Bigger Unknown 145
- 3.5 *Compare* Problems: Smaller Unknown 151
- 3.6 True or False Equations 157
- 3.7 Find Numbers That Make 10 163
- 3.8 Fact Families 169

Performance Task: Baking 175
Game: Number Land 176
Chapter Practice 177
Cumulative Practice 181

Number Land

To Play: Put the Addition and Subtraction Cards in a pile. Start at Newton. Take turns drawing a card and moving your piece to the missing number in the equation. Repeat this process until a player gets back to Newton.

Add Numbers within 20

	Vocabulary	186
■ 4.1	Add Doubles from 6 to 10	187
■ 4.2	Use Doubles within 20	193
■ 4.3	Count On to Add within 20	199
■ 4.4	Add Three Numbers	205
■ 4.5	Add Three Numbers by Making a 10	211
■ 4.6	Add 9	217
■ 4.7	Make a 10 to Add	223
■ 4.8	Problem Solving: Addition within 20	229
	Performance Task: Weather	235
	Game: Roll and Cover	236
	Chapter Practice	237

Subtract Numbers within 20

	Vocabulary	242
■ 5.1	Count Back to Subtract within 20	243
■ 5.2	Use Addition to Subtract within 20	249
■ 5.3	Subtract 9	255
■ 5.4	Get to 10 to Subtract	261
■ 5.5	More True or False Equations	267
■ 5.6	Make True Equations	273
■ 5.7	Problem Solving: Subtraction within 20	279
	Performance Task: Bees	285
	Game: Three in a Row: Subtraction	286
	Chapter Practice	287

■ Major Topic
■ Supporting Topic
■ Additional Topic

6 Count and Write Numbers to 120

	Vocabulary	292
6.1	Count to 120 by Ones	293
6.2	Count to 120 by Tens	299
6.3	Compose Numbers 11 to 19	305
6.4	Tens	311
6.5	Tens and Ones	317
6.6	Make Quick Sketches	323
6.7	Understand Place Value	329
6.8	Write Numbers in Different Ways	335
6.9	Count and Write Numbers to 120	341
	Performance Task: Fundraiser	347
	Game: Drop and Build	348
	Chapter Practice	349

7 Compare Two-Digit Numbers

	Vocabulary	354
7.1	Compare Numbers 11 to 19	355
7.2	Compare Numbers	361
7.3	Compare Numbers Using Place Value	367
7.4	Compare Numbers Using Symbols	373
7.5	Compare Numbers Using a Number Line	379
7.6	1 More, 1 Less; 10 More, 10 Less	385
	Performance Task: Toy Drive	391
	Game: Number Boss	392
	Chapter Practice	393
	Cumulative Practice	397

Let's learn how to compare two-digit numbers!

xxi

Add and Subtract Tens

	Vocabulary	402
■ 8.1	Mental Math: 10 More	403
■ 8.2	Mental Math: 10 Less	409
■ 8.3	Add Tens	415
■ 8.4	Add Tens Using a Number Line	421
■ 8.5	Subtract Tens	427
■ 8.6	Subtract Tens Using a Number Line	433
■ 8.7	Use Addition to Subtract Tens	439
■ 8.8	Add Tens to a Number	445

Performance Task: Motion ... 451
Game: 10 More or 10 Less ... 452
Chapter Practice ... 453

Add Two-Digit Numbers

	Vocabulary	458
■ 9.1	Add Tens and Ones	459
■ 9.2	Add Tens and Ones Using a Number Line	465
■ 9.3	Make a 10 to Add	471
■ 9.4	Add Two-Digit Numbers	477
■ 9.5	Practice Addition Strategies	483
■ 9.6	Problem Solving: Addition	489

Performance Task: Games ... 495
Game: Race for 100 ... 496
Chapter Practice ... 497

■ Major Topic
■ Supporting Topic
■ Additional Topic

xxii

10 Measure and Compare Lengths

Vocabulary 502
- 10.1 Order Objects by Length 503
- 10.2 Compare Lengths Indirectly 509
- 10.3 Measure Lengths 515
- 10.4 Measure More Lengths 521
- 10.5 Solve *Compare* Problems Involving Length 527

Performance Task: Maps 533
Game: Fish Measurement 534
Chapter Practice 535

Think and Grow

Use color tiles to **measure** lengths of objects.

Do not leave gaps or overlap the tiles.

length unit

about __4__ color tiles

xxiii

Represent and Interpret Data

Vocabulary	540
11.1 Sort and Organize Data	541
11.2 Read and Interpret Picture Graphs	547
11.3 Read and Interpret Bar Graphs	553
11.4 Represent Data	559
11.5 Solve Problems Involving Data	565
Performance Task: Eye Color	571
Game: Spin and Graph	572
Chapter Practice	573
Cumulative Practice	577

Tell Time

Vocabulary	582
12.1 Tell Time to the Hour	583
12.2 Tell Time to the Half Hour	589
12.3 Tell Time to the Hour and Half Hour	595
12.4 Tell Time Using Analog and Digital Clocks	601
Performance Task: Field Trip	607
Game: Time Flip and Find	608
Chapter Practice	609

■ Major Topic
■ Supporting Topic
■ Additional Topic

13 Two- and Three-Dimensional Shapes

- **Vocabulary** 612
- 13.1 Sort Two-Dimensional Shapes 613
- 13.2 Describe Two-Dimensional Shapes 619
- 13.3 Combine Two-Dimensional Shapes 625
- 13.4 Create More Shapes 631
- 13.5 Take Apart Two-Dimensional Shapes 637
- 13.6 Sort Three-Dimensional Shapes 643
- 13.7 Describe Three-Dimensional Shapes 649
- 13.8 Combine Three-Dimensional Shapes 655
- 13.9 Take Apart Three-Dimensional Shapes 661

Performance Task: Sandcastles 667
Game: Shape Roll and Build 668
Chapter Practice 669

14 Equal Shares

- **Vocabulary** 674
- 14.1 Equal Shares 675
- 14.2 Partition Shapes into Halves 681
- 14.3 Partition Shapes into Fourths 687

Performance Task: Picnic 693
Game: Three in a Row: Equal Shares 694
Chapter Practice 695
Cumulative Practice 697

Glossary A1
Index A11
Reference Sheet A25

Let's learn about equal shares!

xxv

8 Add and Subtract Tens

- How do pinwheels move?
- A pinwheel spins 40 times. Then it spins 20 more times. How many times does it spin in all?

Chapter Learning Target:
Understand adding and subtracting tens.

Chapter Success Criteria:
- I can identify the number ten.
- I can describe what changes when adding or subtracting ten.
- I can model adding and subtracting tens.
- I can use a number line to show adding and subtracting tens.

8 Vocabulary

Review Words
decade numbers
digits

Organize It

Use the review words to complete the graphic organizer.

[   ]

1	2	3	4	5	6	7	8	9	10
11	12	13	14	15	16	17	18	19	20
21	22	23	24	25	26	27	28	29	30
31	32	33	34	35	36	37	38	39	40
41	42	43	44	45	46	47	48	49	50
51	52	53	54	55	56	57	58	59	60
61	62	63	64	65	66	67	68	69	70
71	72	73	74	75	76	77	78	79	80
81	82	83	84	85	86	87	88	89	90
91	92	93	94	95	96	97	98	99	100
101	102	103	104	105	106	107	108	109	110
111	112	113	114	115	116	117	118	119	120

The [   ] of 16 are 1 and 6.

Define It

What am I?

$13 - 3 = B$ $6 - 4 = M$ $4 + 4 = P$ $12 - 8 = R$
$5 + 1 = O$ $1 + 2 = E$ $3 + 2 = L$ $10 - 3 = U$
$5 + 4 = I$ $9 - 8 = N$

| 6 | 8 | 3 | 1 | | 1 | 7 | 2 | 10 | 3 | 4 | | 5 | 9 | 1 | 3 |

Chapter 8 Vocabulary Cards

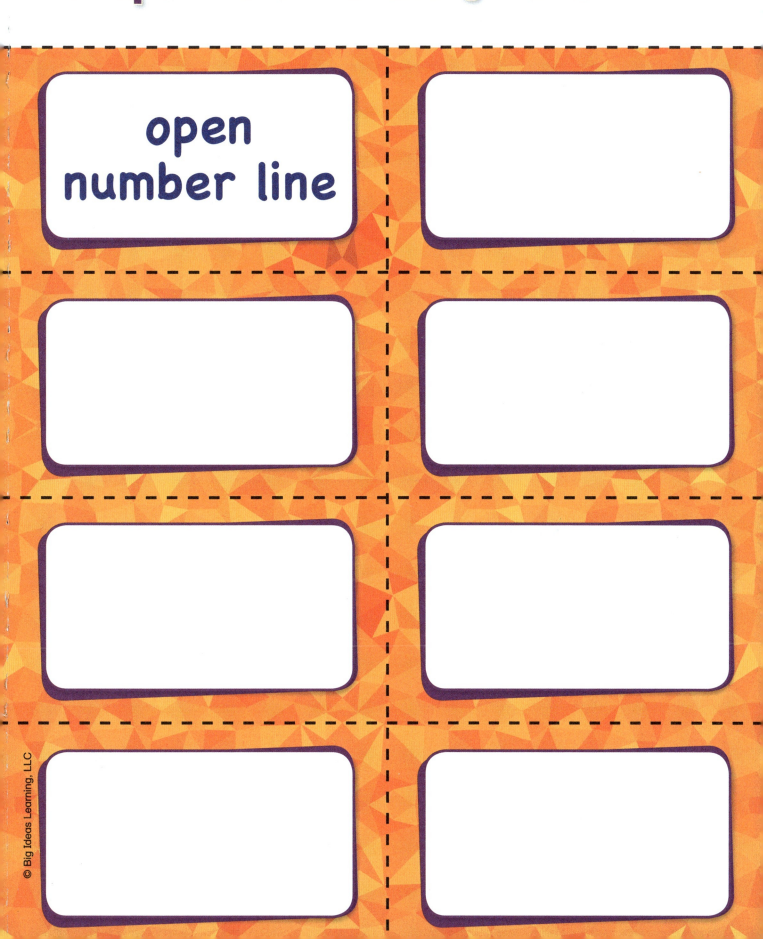

open number line

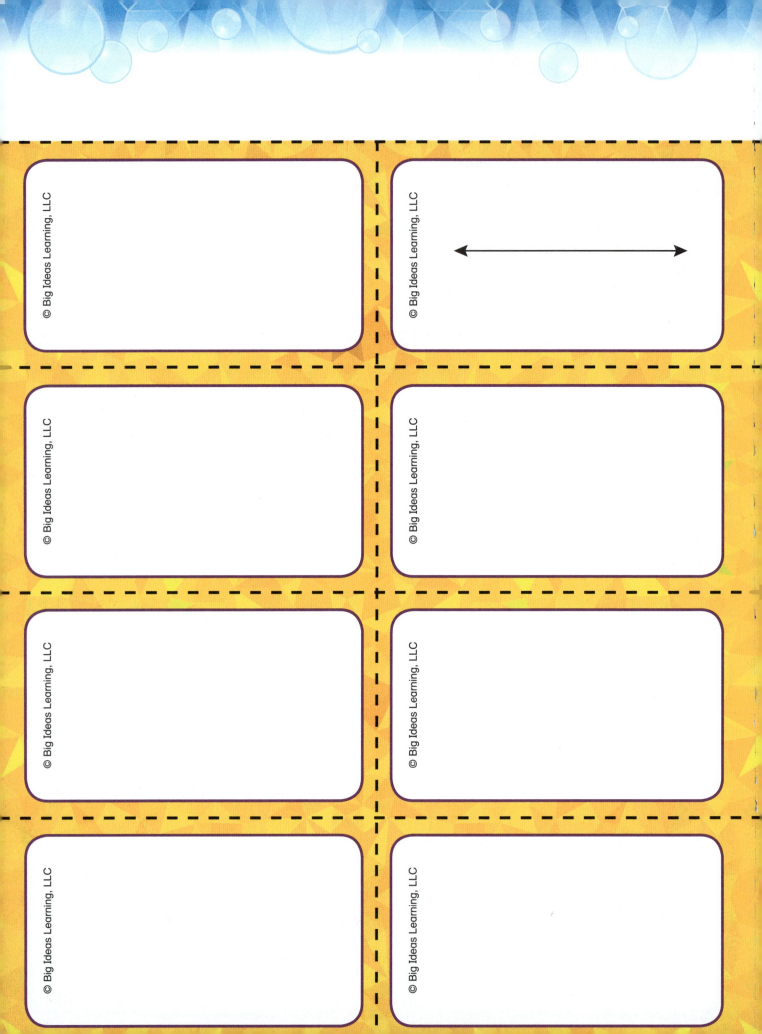

Name _____

Mental Math: 10 More 8.1

Learning Target: Use mental math to add 10.

Explore and Grow

Find each sum. What do you notice?

13 + 10 = ___

39 + 10 = ___

52 + 10 = ___

Chapter 8 | Lesson 1   four hundred three 403

Think and Grow

27 + 10 = __37__

1	2	3	4	5	6	7	8	9	10
11	12	13	14	15	16	17	18	19	20
21	22	23	24	25	26	27	28	29	30
31	32	33	34	35	36	37	38	39	40
41	42	43	44	45	46	47	48	49	50
51	52	53	54	55	56	57	58	59	60
61	62	63	64	65	66	67	68	69	70
71	72	73	74	75	76	77	78	79	80
81	82	83	84	85	86	87	88	89	90
91	92	93	94	95	96	97	98	99	100

Think of moving down 1 row on a hundred chart.

Show and Grow   I can do it!

Use mental math.

1. 14 + 10 = __24__

2. 46 + 10 = ____

3. 83 + 10 = ____

4. 75 + 10 = ____

5. 21 + 10 = ____

6. 60 + 10 = ____

7. 10 + 89 = ____

8. 10 + 68 = ____

404   four hundred four

Name _____

Apply and Grow: Practice

Use mental math.

9. 16 + 10 = 26

10. 63 + 10 = ____

11. 8 + 10 = 18

12. 44 + 10 = ____

13. 19 + 10 = ____

14. 59 + 10 = ____

15. 10 + 22 = ____

16. 10 + 50 = ____

17. 10 + 71 = ____

18. 10 + 38 = ____

19. 55 + ____ = 65

20. 87 + ____ = 97

21. **DIG DEEPER!** Use each number once to complete the equations.

86   76   10   66

____ + 10 = ____   ____ + ____ = 96

Chapter 8 | Lesson 1

Think and Grow: Modeling Real Life

There are 33 students on a bus. 10 more get on. How many students are on the bus now?

Addition equation:

Check Your Work
When adding 10, should the digit in the tens place or the ones place change?

_____ students

Show and Grow I can think deeper!

22. There are 61 tents at a campground. 10 more are put up. How many tents are at the campground now?

Addition equation:

_____ tents

Name _____

Practice 8.1

Learning Target: Use mental math to add 10.

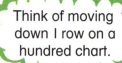
Think of moving down 1 row on a hundred chart.

74 + 10 = **84**

61	62	63	64	65	66	67	68	69	70
71	72	73	74	75	76	77	78	79	80
81	82	83	(84)	85	86	87	88	89	90
91	92	93	94	95	96	97	98	99	100

Use mental math.

1. 30 + 10 = _____

2. 81 + 10 = _____

3. 6 + 10 = _____

4. 57 + 10 = _____

5. 48 + 10 = _____

6. 26 + 10 = _____

7. 10 + 43 = _____

8. 10 + 65 = _____

9. 10 + 82 = _____

10. 10 + 79 = _____

Chapter 8 | Lesson 1

Use mental math.

11. 22 + _____ = 32

12. 85 + _____ = 95

13. 64 + _____ = 74

14. 41 + _____ = 51

15. **DIG DEEPER!** Use each number once to complete the equations.

25   10   15   35

10 + _____ = _____   25 + _____ = _____

16. **Modeling Real Life** There are 42 teachers at a school. The school hires 10 more. How many teachers are there now?

_____ teachers

Review & Refresh

17.

10 less than 87 is _____.

18.

1 less than 33 is _____.

408 four hundred eight

Name _____

Learning Target: Use mental math to subtract 10.

Mental Math: 10 Less   **8.2**

 Explore and Grow

Find each difference. What do you notice?

33 − 10 = ___

67 − 10 = ___

82 − 10 = ___

Chapter 8 | Lesson 2

Think and Grow

36 − 10 = 26

1	2	3	4	5	6	7	8	9	10
11	12	13	14	15	16	17	18	19	20
21	22	23	24	25	26	27	28	29	30
31	32	33	34	35	36	37	38	39	40
41	42	43	44	45	46	47	48	49	50
51	52	53	54	55	56	57	58	59	60
61	62	63	64	65	66	67	68	69	70
71	72	73	74	75	76	77	78	79	80
81	82	83	84	85	86	87	88	89	90
91	92	93	94	95	96	97	98	99	100

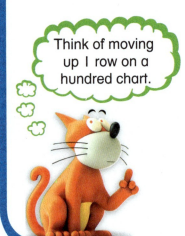

Think of moving up 1 row on a hundred chart.

Show and Grow — I can do it!

Use mental math.

1. 55 − 10 = ____
2. 21 − 10 = ____
3. 18 − 10 = ____
4. 74 − 10 = ____
5. 89 − 10 = ____
6. 72 − 10 = ____

Name _____

Apply and Grow: Practice

Use mental math.

7. $60 - 10 =$ _____

8. $45 - 10 =$ _____

9. $50 - 10 =$ _____

10. $34 - 10 =$ _____

11. $51 - 10 =$ _____

12. $86 - 10 =$ _____

13. $64 - 10 =$ _____

14. $97 - 10 =$ _____

15. $28 - 10 =$ _____

16. $73 - 10 =$ _____

17. _____ $- 10 = 22$

18. _____ $- 10 = 80$

19. **YOU BE THE TEACHER** Is Newton correct? Explain.

$94 - 10 \stackrel{?}{=} 84$

Chapter 8 | Lesson 2

four hundred eleven 411

Think and Grow: Modeling Real Life

You want to ride all 47 rides at an amusement park. You ride 10 of them. How many rides are left?

Subtraction equation:

_____ rides

Show and Grow I can think deeper!

20. You want to try all 65 flavors at a frozen yogurt shop. You try 10 of them. How many flavors are left?

    Subtraction equation:

_____ flavors

Name _____

Practice 8.2

Learning Target: Use mental math to subtract 10.

Think of moving up 1 row on a hundred chart.

83 − 10 = **73**

61	62	63	64	65	66	67	68	69	70
71	72	(73)	74	75	76	77	78	79	80
81	82	83	84	85	86	87	88	89	90
91	92	93	94	95	96	97	98	99	100

Use mental math.

1. 12 − 10 = ____

2. 49 − 10 = ____

3. 37 − 10 = ____

4. 26 − 10 = ____

5. 40 − 10 = ____

6. 62 − 10 = ____

7. 88 − 10 = ____

8. 91 − 10 = ____

9. ____ − 10 = 15

10. ____ − 10 = 77

Chapter 8 | Lesson 2   four hundred thirteen **413**

11. **YOU BE THE TEACHER** Is Descartes correct? Explain.

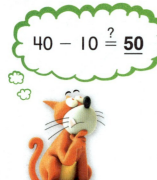

$40 - 10 \stackrel{?}{=} 50$

_____

_____

12. **Modeling Real Life** There are 99 levels in a video game. You complete 10 of them. How many are left?

_____ levels

13. **Communicate Clearly** How is subtracting 10 similar to adding 10? How is it different?

_____

_____

Review & Refresh

14. A group of students are at the arcade. 4 of them leave. There are 5 left. How many students were there to start?

_____ students

Name _____

Learning Target: Add tens.

Add Tens 8.3

 Explore and Grow

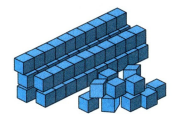

Model each problem. How are the problems alike? How are they different?

3 + 2 = 5

30 + 20 = 5

Chapter 8 | Lesson 3
four hundred fifteen 415

Think and Grow

Look at the tens digits. 2 + 5 = 7, so 2 tens + 5 tens = 7 tens.

20 + 50 = ?

7 tens is 70.

__2__ tens + __5__ tens = __7__ tens

So,   20   +   50   = __70__.

Show and Grow — I can do it!

1. 40 + 50 = ?

   _____ tens + _____ tens = _____ tens

   So, 40 + 50 = _____.

2. 30 + 30 = ?

   _____ tens + _____ tens = _____ tens

   So, 30 + 30 = _____.

Name _____

 **Apply and Grow: Practice**

3. 20 + 40 = ?

_____ tens + _____ tens = _____ tens

So, 20 + 40 = _____.

4. 50 + 30 = ?

_____ tens + _____ tens = _____ tens

So, 50 + 30 = _____.

5. 40 + 10 = _____

6. 70 + 20 = _____

7. 30 + 40 = _____

8. 20 + 60 = _____

9. _____ + 10 = 40

10. _____ + 60 = 90

11. **DIG DEEPER!** Which choices match the model?

50

20 + 30

2 tens + 3 ones

1 ten + 4 tens

Chapter 8 | Lesson 3

four hundred seventeen **417**

Think and Grow: Modeling Real Life

One tray has 20 meatballs. Another tray has the same number of meatballs. How many meatballs are there in all?

Model:

Addition equation:

_____ meatballs

Show and Grow I can think deeper!

12. One box has 40 bags of pretzels. Another box has the same number of bags. How many bags are there in all?

Model:

Addition equation:

_____ bags

Name _____

Practice  **8.3**

Learning Target: Add tens.

$60 + 20 = ?$

 8 tens is 80.

__6__ tens + __2__ tens = __8__ tens

So,   60   +   20   = __80__.

1. $20 + 70 = ?$

_____ tens + _____ tens = _____ tens

So, $20 + 70 =$ _____.

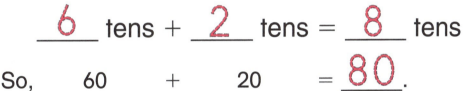

2. $50 + 30 = ?$

_____ tens + _____ tens = _____ tens

So, $50 + 30 =$ _____.

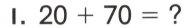

3. $60 + 20 =$ _____

4. $40 + 40 =$ _____

Chapter 8 | Lesson 3

four hundred nineteen

5. ___ + 40 = 50

6. ___ + 30 = 60

7. ___ + 20 = 70

8. ___ + 50 = 90

9. **DIG DEEPER!** Which choices match the model?

3 tens + 4 ones

5 tens + 2 tens

60

30 + 40

10. **Modeling Real Life** One magic set has 30 pieces. Another set has the same number of pieces. How many pieces are there in all?

___ pieces

Review & Refresh

11. ___ = 6 + 5

12. ___ = 3 + 17

13. ___ = 11 + 5

14. ___ = 5 + 9

Name _____

Learning Target: Use an open number line to add tens.

Add Tens Using a Number Line

Explore and Grow

Write the missing numbers. How do the hops help you solve?

$$30 + 20 = \underline{}$$

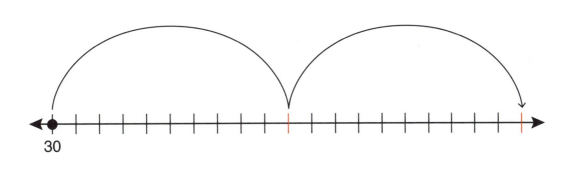

Chapter 8 | Lesson 4
four hundred twenty-one 421

Think and Grow

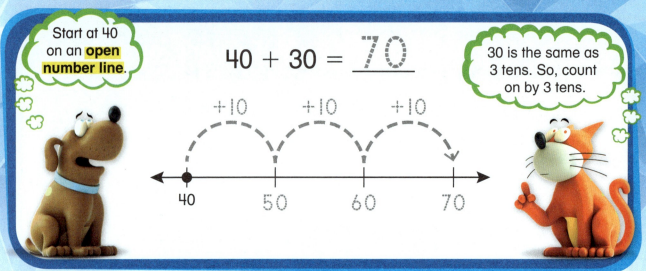

Start at 40 on an **open number line**.

40 + 30 = 70

30 is the same as 3 tens. So, count on by 3 tens.

Show and Grow I can do it!

1. 50 + 40 = ____

2. 60 + 20 = ____

Name _____

Apply and Grow: Practice

3. 40 + 20 = _____

4. 50 + 30 = _____

5. 60 + 40 = _____

6. 20 + 50 = _____

7. **Structure** Write an equation that matches the number line.

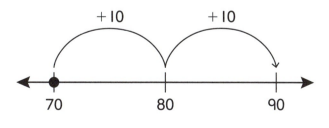

_____ + _____ = _____

Chapter 8 | Lesson 4   four hundred twenty-three   **423**

Think and Grow: Modeling Real Life

You have 20 cans. You collect 20 more cans. Your friend collects 45 cans in all. Who collects more cans?

Model:

⟵——————————⟶

Addition equation: _____

Compare: _____ ◯ _____

Who collects more cans?   You   Friend

Show and Grow — I can think deeper!

8. Your class makes 62 paper airplanes. Your friend's class makes 30 small airplanes and 30 large airplanes. Whose class makes more airplanes?

Model:

⟵——————————⟶

Addition equation: _____

Compare: _____ ◯ _____

Whose class makes more airplanes?   Your class   Friend's class

Name _____

Practice 8.4

Learning Target: Use an open number line to add tens.

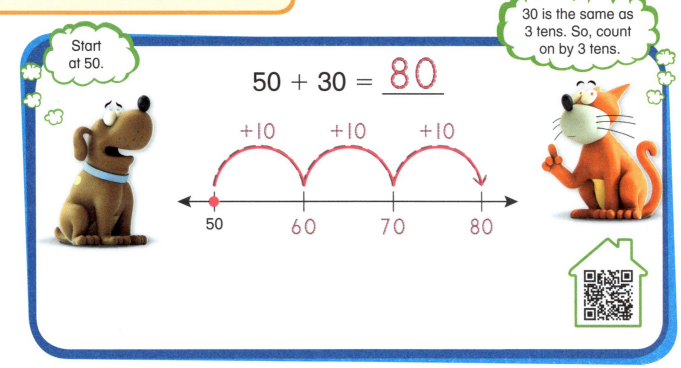

$50 + 30 =$ __80__

1. $60 + 30 =$ _____

2. $20 + 20 =$ _____

3. $30 + 70 =$ _____

Chapter 8 | Lesson 4

4. **Structure** Write an equation that matches the number line.

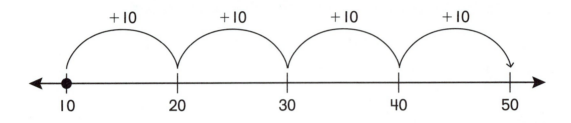

_____ + _____ = _____

5. **Modeling Real Life** You make 39 snow bricks. Your friend makes 20 small snow bricks and 30 large snow bricks. Who makes more snow bricks?

Who makes more snow bricks?   You   Friend

6. **DIG DEEPER!** Write an equation with a sum of 60.

_____ + _____ = _____

Review & Refresh

7. Count by tens to write the missing numbers.

49, _____, _____, _____, _____, _____

Name _____

Learning Target: Subtract tens.

Subtract Tens 8.5

 Explore and Grow

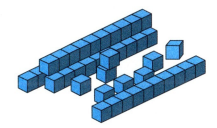

Model each problem. How are the problems alike? How are they different?

5 − 2 = ____

50 − 20 = ____

 **Reasoning**
How does knowing the difference of 5 − 2 help you know the difference of 50 − 20?

Chapter 8 | **Lesson 5**

four hundred twenty-seven 427

Think and Grow

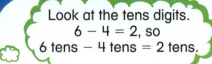

Look at the tens digits.
6 − 4 = 2, so
6 tens − 4 tens = 2 tens.

60 − 40 = ?

2 tens is 20.

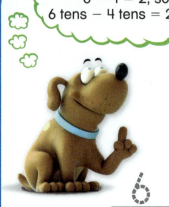

__6__ tens − __4__ tens = __2__ tens

So,   60   −   40   = __20__.

Show and Grow — I can do it!

1. 70 − 30 = ?

   ____ tens − ____ tens = ____ tens

   So, 70 − 30 = ____.

2. 40 − 20 = ____

   ____ tens − ____ tens = ____ tens

   So, 40 − 20 = ____.

Name _____

Apply and Grow: Practice

3. 90 − 30 = ?

_____ tens − _____ tens = _____ tens

So, 90 − 30 = _____.

4. 50 − 10 = ?

_____ tens − _____ ten = _____ tens

So, 50 − 10 = _____.

5. 30 − 20 = _____

6. 40 − 40 = _____

7. 80 − 50 = _____

8. 90 − 70 = _____

9. 20 − _____ = 10

10. 50 − _____ = 20

11. **DIG DEEPER!** Which choices match the model?

50 − 30   80 − 30

5 tens − 3 tens   8 tens − 3 tens

Chapter 8 | Lesson 5   four hundred twenty-nine   429

Think and Grow: Modeling Real Life

You have 80 math problems. You have 40 fewer spelling words. How many spelling words do you have?

Model:

Subtraction equation:

_____ spelling words

Show and Grow — I can think deeper!

12. There are 60 students in a play. A football team has 30 fewer students. How many students are on the football team?

    Model:

    Subtraction equation:

    _____ students

Name _____

Practice 

Learning Target: Subtract tens.

Look at the tens digits.
9 − 6 = 3, so
9 tens − 6 tens = 3 tens.

90 − 60 = ?

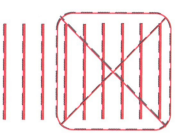

3 tens is 30.

__9__ tens − __6__ tens = __3__ tens

So,   90   −   60   = __30__.

1. 70 − 50 = ?

   ____ tens − ____ tens = ____ tens

   So, 70 − 50 = ____.

2. 60 − 20 = ?

   ____ tens − ____ tens = ____ tens

   So, 60 − 20 = ____.

3. 60 − 60 = ____

4. 30 − 10 = ____

Chapter 8 | Lesson 5   four hundred thirty-one   431

5. 70 – ____ = 0

6. 50 – ____ = 40

7. 40 – ____ = 20

8. 90 – ____ = 50

9. **DIG DEEPER!** Which choices match the model?

90 – 50   40 – 5

4 tens – 5 ones   9 tens – 5 tens

10. **Modeling Real Life** There are 40 chairs in the library. There are 30 fewer tables than chairs. How many tables are there?

____ tables

Review & Refresh

11. 11 – 7 = ____

12. 16 – 8 = ____

13. 15 – 8 = ____

14. 18 – 9 = ____

Name _____

Subtract Tens Using a Number Line

Learning Target: Use an open number line to subtract tens.

Explore and Grow

Write the missing numbers. How do the hops help you solve?

$$40 - 20 = \underline{}$$

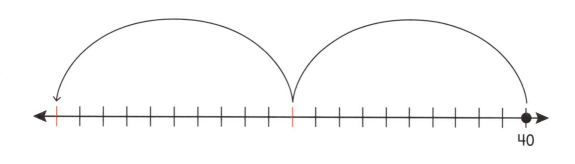

_____   _____

Find a Rule
When using a number line to subtract, will you always move to the left or to the right? Why?

Chapter 8 | Lesson 6

four hundred thirty-three 433

Think and Grow

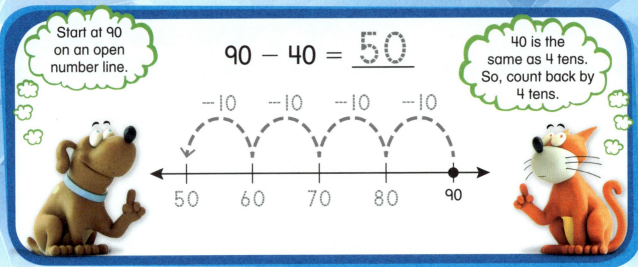

Show and Grow — I can do it!

1. 80 − 50 = _____

2. 70 − 30 = _____

Name _____

✓ Apply and Grow: Practice

3. 60 − 20 = _____

4. 40 − 30 = _____

5. 90 − 40 = _____

6. 90 − 70 = _____

7. **MP Structure** Write the equation that matches the number line.

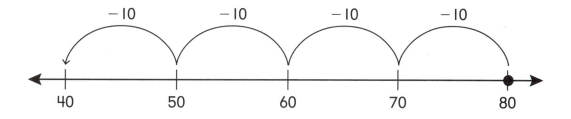

_____ − _____ = _____

Think and Grow: Modeling Real Life

You have a bucket of 80 golf balls. You hit 60 of them. Your friend has 28 golf balls left. Who has more golf balls left?

Model:

⟵——————————————⟶

Subtraction equation: _____

Compare: _____ ◯ _____

Who has more golf balls left?   You   Friend

Show and Grow   I can think deeper!

8. Pack A has 50 batteries. 40 of them have been used. Pack B has 15 batteries. Which pack has more batteries left?

Model:

⟵——————————————⟶

Subtraction equation: _____

Compare: _____ ◯ _____

Which pack has more batteries left?   Pack A   Pack B

Name _____

Practice 8.6

Learning Target: Use an open number line to subtract tens.

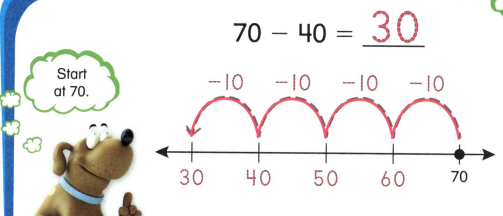

$70 - 40 = \underline{30}$

1. $50 - 30 = \underline{}$

2. $80 - 60 = \underline{}$

3. $90 - 20 = \underline{}$

Chapter 8 | Lesson 6   four hundred thirty-seven   437

4. **Structure** Write the equation that matches the number line.

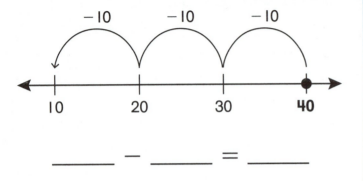

_____ − _____ = _____

5. **Choose Tools** Do you prefer to use models or a number line to subtract tens? Explain.

_____

_____

_____

6. **Modeling Real Life** You have 80 raffle tickets and give away 30 of them. Your friend has 47 raffle tickets. Who has more raffle tickets?

Who has more raffle tickets?   You   Friend

Review & Refresh

7. $13 − 8 = ?$

Think $8 + \underline{} = 13$.

So, $13 − 8 = \underline{}$.

8. $15 − 7 = ?$

Think $7 + \underline{} = 15$.

So, $15 − 7 = \underline{}$.

Name _____

Use Addition to Subtract Tens 8.7

Learning Target: Use addition to subtract tens.

Explore and Grow

Complete each equation. What do you notice?

20

20 + ___ = 50

50

50 − 20 = ___

Chapter 8 | Lesson 7   four hundred thirty-nine 439

Think and Grow

$80 - 50 = ?$

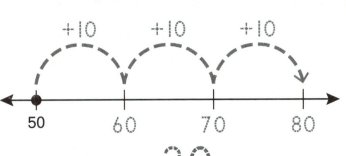

Think $50 +$ __30__ $= 80$.

So, $80 - 50 =$ __30__.

Show and Grow I can do it!

1. $90 - 70 = ?$

Think $70 +$ _____ $= 90$.

So, $90 - 70 =$ _____.

2. $60 - 30 = ?$

Think $30 +$ _____ $= 60$.

So, $60 - 30 =$ _____.

Name _____

 **Apply and Grow: Practice**

3. 50 − 30 = ?

30

Think 30 + ____ = 50.   So, 50 − 30 = ____.

4. 70 − 20 = ?

Think 20 + ____ = 70.   So, 70 − 20 = ____.

5. 90 − 50 = ?

Think 50 + ____ = 90.   So, 90 − 50 = ____.

6. **Structure** Match the related addition and subtraction equations.

60 + 10 = 70   70 − 50 = 20

50 + 10 = 60   70 − 60 = 10

50 + 20 = 70   60 − 50 = 10

Chapter 8 | Lesson 7   four hundred forty-one 441

Think and Grow: Modeling Real Life

A dentist has 40 toothbrushes. She gives away 20 of them. How many toothbrushes does she have left?

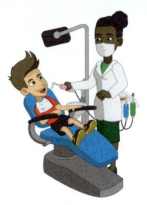

Model:

⟵—————————————⟶

Subtraction equation:

_____ toothbrushes

Show and Grow — I can think deeper!

7. An art room has 70 bottles of glitter. 30 have been used. How many bottles are left?

Model:

⟵—————————————⟶

Subtraction equation:

_____ bottles

Name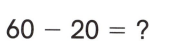

Practice 8.7

Learning Target: Use addition to subtract tens.

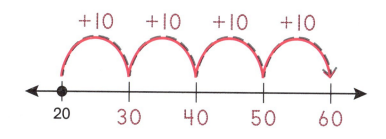

60 − 20 = ?

Start at 20. Count on by tens to get to 60.

Think 20 + **40** = 60.

So, 60 − 20 = **40**.

1. 70 − 40 = ?

Think 40 + _____ = 70.   So, 70 − 40 = _____.

2. 90 − 30 = ?

Think 30 + _____ = 90.   So, 90 − 30 = _____.

Chapter 8 | Lesson 7   four hundred forty-three   443

3. **Structure** Match the related addition and subtraction equations.

$$30 + 10 = 40 \qquad 40 + 10 = 50 \qquad 30 + 20 = 50$$

$$50 - 40 = 10 \qquad 50 - 30 = 20 \qquad 40 - 30 = 10$$

4. **Modeling Real Life** Newton has 80 newspapers to deliver. He delivers 50 of them. How many newspapers does he have left?

_____ newspapers

5. **DIG DEEPER!** Write the missing number.

$$60 - \text{🌸} = 10 \qquad\qquad \text{❤️} - 40 = 40$$

$$\text{❤️} - \text{🌸} = \underline{}$$

Review & Refresh

6. Make quick sketches to compare the numbers.

43 is greater than 34.
is less than

Name _____

Add Tens to a Number 8.8

Learning Target: Add tens to a number.

Explore and Grow

Find each sum. What do you notice?

1	2	3	4	5	6	7	8	9	10
11	12	13	14	15	16	17	18	19	20
21	22	23	24	25	26	27	28	29	30
31	32	33	34	35	36	37	38	39	40
41	42	43	44	45	46	47	48	49	50
51	52	53	54	55	56	57	58	59	60

15 + 10 = ____   27 + 10 = ____

15 + 20 = ____   27 + 20 = ____

15 + 30 = ____   27 + 30 = ____

Chapter 8 | Lesson 8   four hundred forty-five   445

Think and Grow

$16 + 30 = \underline{46}$

Add the tens. Keep 6 for the ones digit.

One Way: Make a quick sketch.

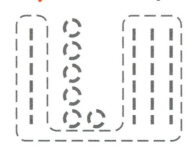

Another Way: Use an open number line.

Start at 16. Count on by 3 tens.

Show and Grow I can do it!

1. $23 + 50 = \underline{}$

2. $6 + 70 = \underline{}$

446 four hundred forty-six

Name _____

Apply and Grow: Practice

3. 27 + 40 = _____

4. 8 + 80 = _____

5. 60 + 35 = _____

6. 30 + 44 = _____

7. _____ = 33 + 20

8. _____ = 70 + 22

9.  Is Newton correct? Explain.

_____

_____

_____

_____

Chapter 8 | Lesson 8

Think and Grow: Modeling Real Life

You count 8 birds on your way to school. You count 40 more on your way home. Your friend counts 45 birds in all. Who counts more birds?

Model:

Addition equation:

Compare: _____ ◯ _____

Who counts more birds?   You   Friend

Show and Grow — I can think deeper!

10. You make 21 snowballs. Your friend makes 11 small snowballs and 20 large snowballs. Who makes more snowballs?

Model:

Addition equation:

Compare: _____ ◯ _____

Who makes more snowballs?   You   Friend

Name _____

Practice 8.8

Learning Target: Add tens to a number.

12 + 20 = __32__

One Way: Make a quick sketch.

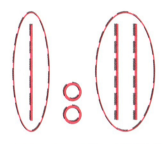

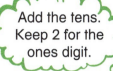
Add the tens. Keep 2 for the ones digit.

Another Way: Use an open number line.

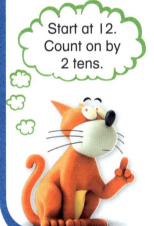
Start at 12. Count on by 2 tens.

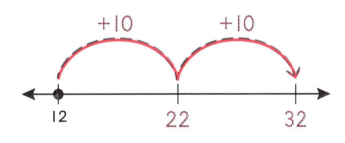

1. 19 + 40 = _____

2. 60 + 23 = _____

3. _____ = 5 + 90

4. _____ = 37 + 30

5. **Modeling Real Life** You have 24 glow sticks and buy 40 more. Your friend has 66 glow sticks. Who has more glow sticks?

Who has more glow sticks?   You   Friend

6. **Modeling Real Life** You earn 54 points in a video game. Your friend earns some points. You and your friend have a total of 94 points. How many points does your friend earn?

_____ points

Review & Refresh

7. Circle the solid shapes that stack.

Name _____

Performance Task 8

1. The tables show the numbers of seconds 3 pinwheels and 3 tops spin.

Pinwheel	Seconds
Red	40
Yellow	90
Blue	

Top	Seconds
Red	
Yellow	50
Blue	36

a. How many more seconds does the yellow top spin than the red pinwheel?

_____ seconds

b. The red pinwheel spins 30 fewer seconds than the red top. How long does the red top spin?

_____ seconds

c. The blue pinwheel and the blue top spin for 96 seconds in all. How long does the blue pinwheel spin?

_____ seconds

d. Which pinwheel spins the longest?

    Red   Yellow   Blue

10 More or 10 Less

To Play: Players take turns. On your turn, roll a die to see how many tens you have. Decide whether you want to add 10 to your number or subtract 10 from your number. Place a counter on your sum or difference. Once the board is covered, clear the board and play again.

Name _____

Chapter Practice 8

8.1 Mental Math: 10 More

Use mental math.

1. 58 + 10 = _____
2. 15 + 10 = _____
3. 29 + 10 = _____
4. 41 + 10 = _____
5. 10 + 7 = _____
6. 10 + 36 = _____
7. 84 + _____ = 94
8. 47 + _____ = 57

8.2 Mental Math: 10 Less

Use mental math.

9. 24 − 10 = _____
10. 78 − 10 = _____
11. 31 − 10 = _____
12. 95 − 10 = _____
13. _____ − 10 = 7
14. _____ − 10 = 43

Chapter 8 four hundred fifty-three 453

8.3 Add Tens

15. 60 + 20 = ?

_____ tens + _____ tens = _____ tens

So, 60 + 20 = _____.

16. 30 + 50 = _____

17. _____ + 30 = 90

8.4 Add Tens Using a Number Line

18. 50 + 40 = _____

19. **Structure** Write an equation that matches the number line.

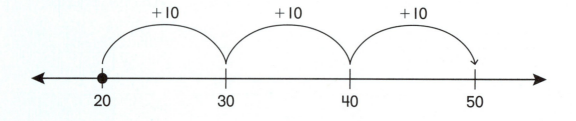

_____ + _____ = _____

8.5 Subtract Tens

20. 90 − 40 = ?

_____ tens − _____ tens = _____ tens

So, 90 − 40 = _____.

21. 70 − 40 = _____

22. 80 − _____ = 60

8.6 Subtract Tens Using a Number Line

23.

60 − 40 = _____

24. **MP Structure** Write the equation that matches the number line.

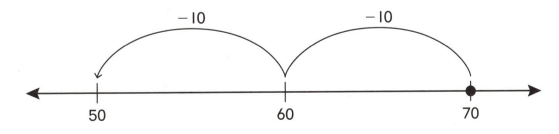

_____ − _____ = _____

Chapter 8   four hundred fifty-five   **455**

8.7 Use Addition to Subtract Tens

25. 80 − 60 = ?

60

Think 60 + _____ = 80.   So, 80 − 60 = _____.

26. **Modeling Real Life** A mail carrier has 90 packages to deliver. She delivers 60 of them. How many packages are left?

_____ packages

8.8 Add Tens to a Number

27. 27 + 50 = _____   **28.** _____ = 80 + 12

9 Add Two-Digit Numbers

- What are your favorite sports?
- You dribble a basketball 18 times with your right hand and 32 times with your left hand. How many times do you dribble the basketball in all?

Chapter Learning Target:
Understand adding two-digit numbers.

Chapter Success Criteria:
- I can identify two-digit numbers.
- I can describe an addition strategy.
- I can write a sum.
- I can explain the strategy and the sum.

four hundred fifty-seven

Name _____

9 Vocabulary

Review Words
120 chart
column
ones
row
tens

Organize It

Use the review words to complete the graphic organizer.

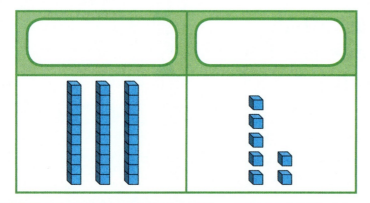

Define It

Use the review words to complete the puzzle.

Across

1. [120 chart grid 1–120]

Down

2. [chart with column 5, 15, 25, 35 highlighted]

3. [chart with row 21, 22, 23, 24, 25 highlighted]

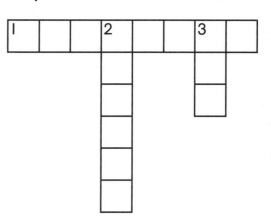

458 four hundred fifty-eight

Name _____

Add Tens and Ones

9.1

Learning Target: Add two numbers by adding the tens and adding the ones.

Show how you can use a model to solve.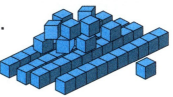

32 + 7 = ___

Tens	Ones

Chapter 9 | Lesson 1   four hundred fifty-nine   459

Think and Grow

$31 + 14 = \underline{45}$

Add the ones. Then add the tens.

Show and Grow — I can do it!

1. $25 + 12 =$ ____

2. $36 + 3 =$ ____

3. $21 + 8 =$ ____

4. $22 + 24 =$ ____

Name _____

Apply and Grow: Practice

5. 34 + 4 = _____

6. 43 + 15 = _____

7. 71 + 20 = _____

8. 93 + 6 = _____

9. 55 + 23 = _____

10. 62 + 32 = _____

11. **Reasoning** Circle the number to complete the equation.

41 + _____ = 46

5   50

Think and Grow: Modeling Real Life

You watch television for 24 minutes in the morning and 32 minutes at night. How many minutes do you spend watching television in all?

Addition equation:

Model:

_____ minutes

Show and Grow — I can think deeper!

12. You do 42 jumping jacks in the morning and 46 at night. How many jumping jacks do you do in all?

    Addition equation:

    Model:

    _____ jumping jacks

Practice 9.1

Learning Target: Add two numbers by adding the tens and adding the ones.

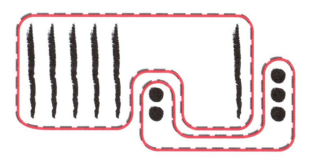

$52 + 13 = \underline{65}$

1. $42 + 7 = \underline{}$

2. $61 + 35 = \underline{}$

3. $74 + 11 = \underline{}$

4. $86 + 2 = \underline{}$

Chapter 9 | Lesson 1   four hundred sixty-three   463

5. **Reasoning** Circle the number to complete the equation.

$$22 + \underline{69} = 92$$

7   **70**

6. **Modeling Real Life** You eat 33 grapes. Your friend eats 23 grapes. How many grapes do you and your friend eat in all?

____ grapes

7. **DIG DEEPER!** What is the greatest number of tens you can add to a two-digit number to get a sum of 35?

Review & Refresh

8. 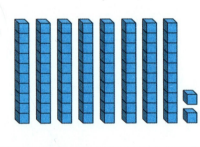 ____ tens and ____ ones is ____.

9. 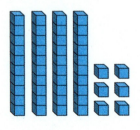 ____ tens and ____ ones is ____.

Name: Brady

Add Tens and Ones Using a Number Line 9.2

Learning Target: Use a number line to add two numbers.

 Explore and Grow

Color to show how you can use the hundred chart to find the sum.

23 + 34 = 57

1	2	3	4	5	6	7	8	9	10
11	12	13	14	15	16	17	18	19	20
21	22	23	24	25	26	27	28	29	30
31	32	33	34	35	36	37	38	39	40
41	42	43	44	45	46	47	48	49	50
51	52	53	54	55	56	57	58	59	60
61	62	63	64	65	66	67	68	69	70
71	72	73	74	75	76	77	78	79	80
81	82	83	84	85	86	87	88	89	90
91	92	93	94	95	96	97	98	99	100

Chapter 9 | Lesson 2

four hundred sixty-five

Think and Grow

One Way:

$26 + 32 = ?$

Start at 26. Count by tens, then by ones.

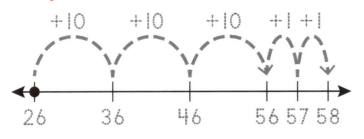

Another Way:

You can also count by ones, then by tens.

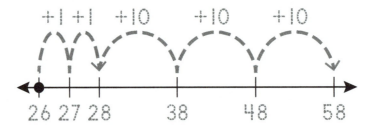

$26 + 32 = \underline{58}$

Show and Grow I can do it!

1. $22 + 7 =$ _____

2. $35 + 41 =$ _____

Apply and Grow: Practice

3. 53 + 40 = _____

4. 82 + 12 = _____

5. 48 + 31 = _____

6. **Structure** Write an equation that matches the number line.

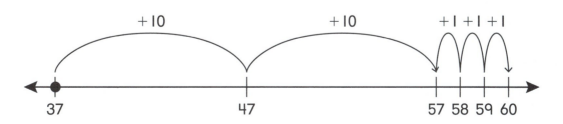

_____ + _____ = _____

Chapter 9 | Lesson 2

Think and Grow: Modeling Real Life

The home team scores 37 points. The visiting team scores 22 more. How many points does the visiting team score?

Addition equation:

Model:

⟵————————————⟶

_____ points

Show and Grow   I can think deeper!

7. Your friend scores 63 points. You score 25 more than your friend. How many points do you score?

Addition equation:

Model:

⟵————————————⟶

_____ points

Name _____

Practice 9.2

Learning Target: Use a number line to add two numbers.

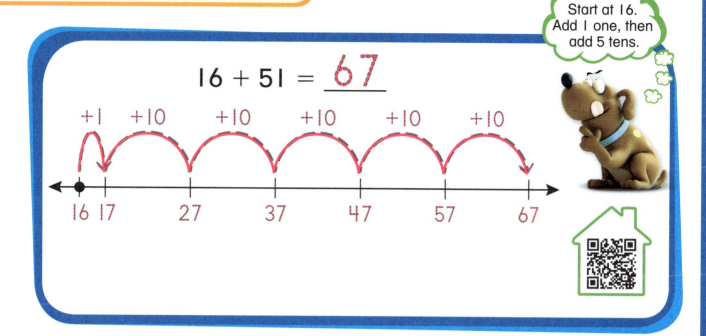

1. 13 + 60 = _____

13

2. 81 + 18 = _____

3. 56 + 42 = _____

Chapter 9 | Lesson 2

4. **Structure** Write an equation that matches the number line.

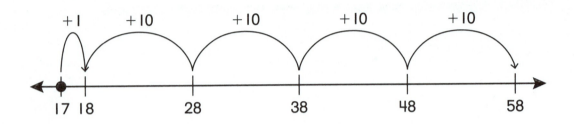

_____ + _____ = _____

5. **Modeling Real Life** There are 36 black keys on a piano. There are 16 more white keys than black keys. How many white keys are there?

_____ white keys

6. **Choose Tools** Do you prefer to use models or a number line to add two numbers? Explain.

_____

_____

Review & Refresh

7. $3 + 7 + 4 =$ _____

8. $4 + 5 + 6 =$ _____

Name _____

Make a 10 to Add 9.3

Learning Target: Make a 10 to add a one-digit number and a two-digit number.

Explore and Grow

How can you use the model to solve?

$$38 + 6 = \underline{}$$

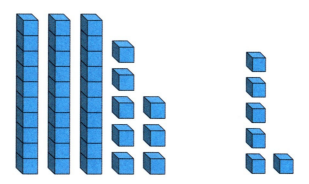

Maintain Accuracy How many ones are in 1 ten? How many tens can you make?

Chapter 9 | Lesson 3

Think and Grow

$38 + 5 = 43$

Make a 10? (Yes)   No

When there are 10 or more ones, make a ten.

$38 + 5$
$38 + 2 + 3$
$40 + 3$

$25 + 4 = 29$

Make a 10?   Yes   (No)

Analyze a Problem
Why don't you need to make a 10 here?

Show and Grow   I can do it!

1. $41 + 7 = $ _____

Make a 10?   Yes   No

2. $56 + 8 = $ _____

Make a 10?   Yes   No

Name _____

✓ Apply and Grow: Practice

3. 72 + 4 = ____

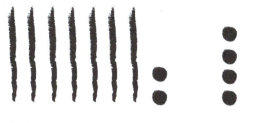

Make a 10?   Yes   No

4. 63 + 9 = ____

Make a 10?   Yes   No

5. 14 + 6 = ____

Make a 10?   Yes   No

6. 27 + 5 = ____

Make a 10?   Yes   No

7. 46 + 7 = ____

Make a 10?   Yes   No

8. 81 + 8 = ____

Make a 10?   Yes   No

Logic Complete.

9.   56 + 6
     56 + ◯ + ◯
         60 + ◯

56 + 6 = ____

10.   39 + 9
     39 + ◯ + ◯
         40 + ◯

39 + 9 = ____

Chapter 9 | Lesson 3   four hundred seventy-three   **473**

Think and Grow: Modeling Real Life

You put 17 puzzle pieces together. There are 7 left. How many puzzle pieces are there in all?

Addition equation:

Model:

Make a 10? Yes No

_____ puzzle pieces

Show and Grow — I can think deeper!

11. You color 46 states. There are 4 left. How many states are there in all?

Addition equation:

Model:

Make a 10? Yes No

_____ states

Name _____

Practice 9.3

Learning Target: Make a 10 to add a one-digit number and a two-digit number.

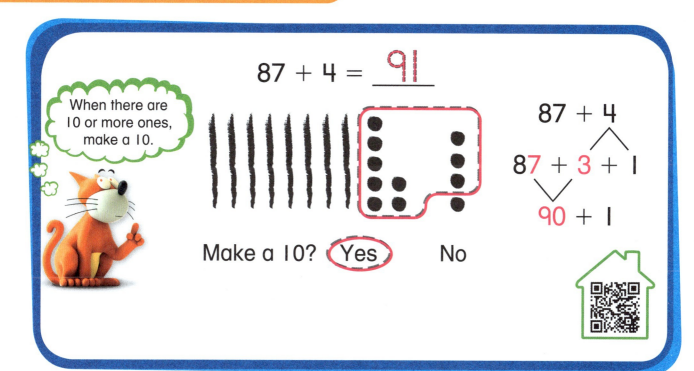

87 + 4 = **91**

When there are 10 or more ones, make a 10.

Make a 10? **Yes**   No

87 + 4
87 + 3 + 1
90 + 1

1. 66 + 5 = ____

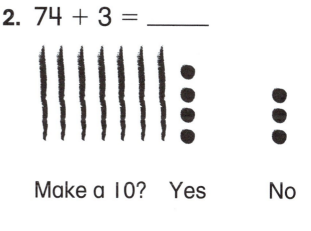

Make a 10?   Yes   No

2. 74 + 3 = ____

Make a 10?   Yes   No

3. 28 + 8 = ____

Make a 10?   Yes   No

4. 52 + 9 = ____

Make a 10?   Yes   No

Chapter 9 | Lesson 3

four hundred seventy-five 475

5. 26 + 7 = _____

Make a 10?   Yes   No

6. 41 + 6 = _____

Make a 10?   Yes   No

7. **Logic** Complete.

37 + 4

37 + ◯ + ◯

40 + ◯

37 + 4 = _____

8. **Modeling Real Life**
A snake lays 24 eggs. Another snake lays 9 eggs. How many eggs are there in all?

_____ eggs

9. **DIG DEEPER!** Find the sums. What is similar about how you find the sums?

36 + 6 = _____   56 + 6 = _____

_____

_____

Review & Refresh

10. Color the shapes that have 4 vertices.

Name _____

Add Two-Digit Numbers 9.4

Learning Target: Use place value to add two numbers.

Show how you can use a model to solve.

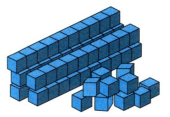

43 + 28 = ____

Tens	Ones

Chapter 9 | Lesson 4

four hundred seventy-seven 477

Think and Grow

Find the number of tens by counting the rods and the group of 10 units.

$26 + 28 = ?$

Find the number of ones by counting the units that are left.

Tens	Ones
26	
28	

Tens	Ones
2	6
2	8
+	
5	4

__5__ tens __4__ ones

Show and Grow — I can do it!

1. $39 + 45 = ?$

Tens	Ones
39	
45	

Tens	Ones
3	9
4	5
+	

_____ tens _____ ones

Name _____

 Apply and Grow: Practice

2. 19 + 35 = ?

Tens	Ones
19	
35	

	Tens	Ones
	1	9
+	3	5

_____ tens _____ ones

3. 43
  + 17

Tens	Ones
+	

4. 67
  + 14

Tens	Ones
+	

5. **YOU BE THE TEACHER** Is the sum correct? Explain.

58
+ 28

76

Tens	Ones
|||||	••• ••• •••
||	••• ••

_____

_____

_____

_____

Chapter 9 | Lesson 4 four hundred seventy-nine 479

Think and Grow: Modeling Real Life

You earn a sticker for every 10 pages you read. You read 34 pages one week and 37 the next. How many stickers do you earn?

Addition problem:

```
   
 + 
___
```

Model:

Tens	Ones

Write the missing numbers:

_____ tens _____ one

_____ stickers

Show and Grow   I can think deeper!

6. You earn a coin for every 10 cans you recycle. You recycle 18 cans one week and 25 the next. How many coins do you earn?

Addition problem:

```
   
 + 
___
```

Model:

Tens	Ones

Write the missing numbers:

_____ tens _____ ones

_____ coins

Name _____

Practice 9.4

Learning Target: Use place value to add two numbers.

16 + 27 = ?

Remember to make a 10 when there are 10 or more ones.

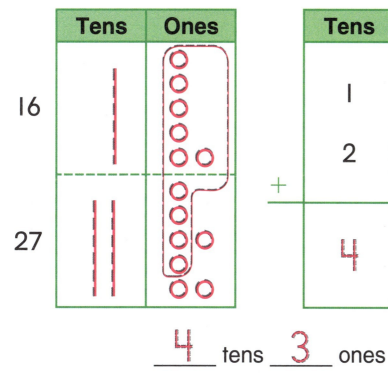

Tens	Ones
1	6
2	7
4	3

+

__4__ tens __3__ ones

1. 57 + 15 = ?

Tens	Ones
57	
15	

Tens	Ones
5	7
1	5

+

_____ tens _____ ones

Chapter 9 | Lesson 4   four hundred eighty-one   481

2. 40
   + 36
   ─────

Tens	Ones

   +

3. 29
   + 52
   ─────

Tens	Ones

   +

4. **DIG DEEPER!** Do you need to use the *make a 10* strategy to find each sum?

   $28 + 34 = ?$ Yes   No $42 + 21 = ?$ Yes   No

   $56 + 15 = ?$ Yes   No $68 + 11 = ?$ Yes   No

5. **Modeling Real Life** You need a box for every 10 muffins you make. You make 33 blueberry muffins and 47 banana muffins. How many boxes do you need?

   _____ boxes

Review & Refresh

6. Is the equation true or false?

   $6 + 9 \stackrel{?}{=} 17 - 1$ $6 + 9:$ $17 - 1:$

   _____ $\stackrel{?}{=}$ _____

   True   False

482   four hundred eighty-two

Name _____

Learning Target: Choose a strategy to add two numbers.

Practice Addition Strategies

Explore and Grow

Show two ways you can find the sum.

23 + 39 = ___

23 + 39 = ___

Chapter 9 | Lesson 5

four hundred eighty-three

Think and Grow

$$29 + 36 = \,?$$

One Way:

$$\begin{array}{r} 29 \\ +\ 36 \\ \hline 65 \end{array}$$

Choose a strategy.

Another Way:

$$29 + 36 = \underline{65}$$

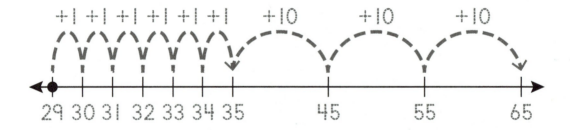

Show and Grow   I can do it!

1. $47 + 24 =$ _____

2. $38 + 43 =$ _____

Name _____

 Apply and Grow: Practice

3. 22 + 18 = _____

_____

4. 57 + 34 = _____

_____

5. 73 + 19 = _____

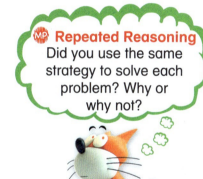

Repeated Reasoning
Did you use the same strategy to solve each problem? Why or why not?

_____

6. 81 + 11 = _____

7. **YOU BE THE TEACHER** Is the sum correct? Explain.

17 + 26 $\stackrel{?}{=}$ **79**

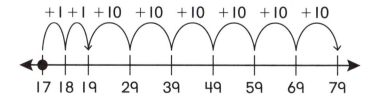

_____

_____

_____

_____

Chapter 9 | Lesson 5   four hundred eighty-five

Think and Grow: Modeling Real Life

You have 48 songs. Your friend has 27 more than you. How many songs does your friend have?

Addition equation:

Model:

_____ songs

Show and Grow   I can think deeper!

8. Your friend sells 56 candles. You sell 35 more than your friend. How many candles do you sell?

   Addition equation:

   Model:

_____ candles

Name _____

Practice 9.5

Learning Target: Choose a strategy to add two numbers.

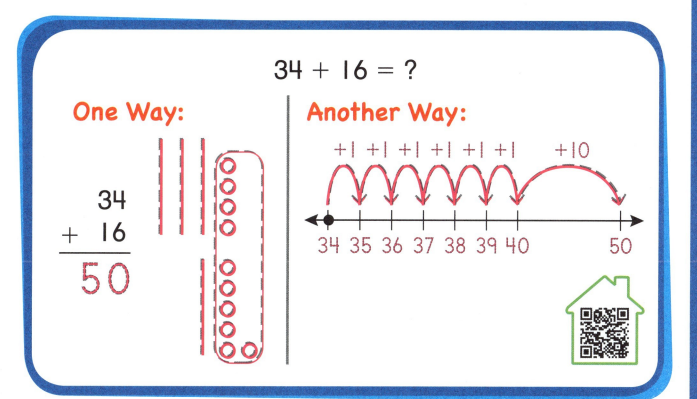

1. 62 + 29 = ____

Communicate Clearly
Which method do you prefer? Why?

2. 84 + 8 = ____

3. 75 + 17 = ____

Chapter 9 | Lesson 5   four hundred eighty-seven **487**

4. **YOU BE THE TEACHER** Is the sum correct? Explain.

    58
  + 33
  ―――
   91

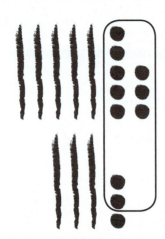

_____

_____

_____

_____

5. **Modeling Real Life** You collect 12 leaves. Your friend collects 26 more than you. How many leaves does your friend collect?

   _____ leaves

6. **Modeling Real Life** You pick 25 oranges. Newton picks 16 oranges and Descartes picks 7 oranges. Do you or Newton and Descartes together pick more oranges? How many more?

   You   Newton and Descartes   _____ more oranges

Review & Refresh

7. Circle the measurable attributes of the table.

length or height   weight   capacity

Name _____

Problem Solving: Addition 9.6

Learning Target: Solve addition word problems.

Explore and Grow

Model the story.

Newton has 15 dog bones. Descartes gives him 8 more. How many dog bones does Newton have now?

_____ dog bones

Chapter 9 | Lesson 6

four hundred eighty-nine 489

Think and Grow

You ride your bike for 28 minutes. Then you ride your scooter. You ride for 44 minutes in all. How long do you ride your scooter?

Circle what you know. Underline what you need to find.

Solve: 28 + ? = 44

Use an open number line.

Start at 28. Count on by tens and ones until you reach 44.

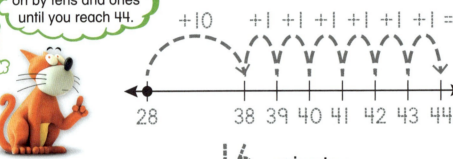

_16_ minutes

Show and Grow   I can do it!

1. You have 49 toy soldiers. You buy some more. Now you have 84. How many toy soldiers did you buy?

Circle what you know: Underline what you need to find.

Solve:

_____ toy soldiers

Name _____

Apply and Grow: Practice

2. You have 55 pounds of dog food and some cat food. You have 63 pounds of pet food in all. How many pounds of cat food do you have?

Circle what you know.

Underline what you need to find.

Solve:

_____ pounds

3. A teacher has 34 erasers. There are 46 fewer erasers than pencils. How many pencils are there?

_____ pencils

4. DIG DEEPER! You have 25 toys. Your friend has more than you. There are more than 60 toys in all. How many toys can your friend have?

29   33   24   38

Chapter 9 | Lesson 6   four hundred ninety-one   491

Think and Grow: Modeling Real Life

You need 60 invitations. You have 36 and buy 36 more. Do you have enough invitations?

Circle what you know.

Underline what you need to find.

Solve:

Compare: _____ ◯ 60   Yes   No

Show and Grow I can think deeper!

5. You need 84 bottles of water. You have 48 and buy 32 more. Do you have enough bottles of water?

Circle what you know.

Underline what you need to find.

Solve:

Compare: _____ ◯ 84   Yes   No

Name _____

Practice 9.6

Learning Target: Solve addition word problems.

You have 23 seashells. You find some more. Now you have 39. How many more seashells did you find?

Circle what you know.

Underline what you need to find.

Solve: 23 + ? = 39

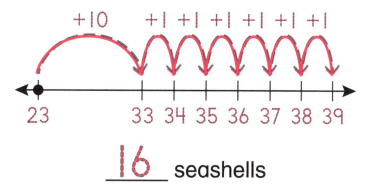

___16___ seashells

1. You have 31 stuffed animals. You and your friend have 60 stuffed animals in all. How many stuffed animals does your friend have?

   _____ stuffed animals

2. A store has 56 shirts. There are 28 fewer shirts than pairs of pants. How many pairs of pants are there?

   _____ pairs of pants

Chapter 9 | Lesson 6   four hundred ninety-three 493

3. **DIG DEEPER!** You have 46 toys. You and your friend have more than 60 toys in all. What is the fewest number of toys your friend can have? Explain.

         13   14   15   16

_____

_____

4. **Modeling Real Life** Newton needs 90 chairs for a party. He has 51. He rents 39 more. Does Newton have enough chairs?

Circle: Yes   No

Review & Refresh

Circle the longer object.

5.

6.

Name _____

Performance Task 9

1. You play a game. Each red ball you collect is worth 10 points. Each yellow ball you collect is worth 1 point.

   a. You collect 3 red balls and 13 yellow balls. How many points do you have?

   _____ points

   b. Your teammates score 38 points and 24 points. How many points do your teammates have in all?

   _____ points

   c. Your team wants to have 100 points. Does your team reach its goal?

   Yes   No

   d. Why do you think a red ball is worth more points?

Chapter 9 four hundred ninety-five 495

Race for 100

To Play: Take turns. On your turn, roll the dice. Find the sum of the numbers and place that many cubes on your mat. If you have 10 or more cubes in the Ones column, exchange 10 cubes for a rod to place in your Tens column. Continue taking turns until someone reaches 100.

Tens	Ones

Name _____

Chapter Practice

9.1 Add Tens and Ones

1. 56 + 3 = _____

2. 22 + 54 = _____

9.2 Add Tens and Ones Using a Number Line

3. 62 + 25 = _____

4. 38 + 51 = _____

Chapter 9   four hundred ninety-seven   497

5. **MP Structure** Write an equation that matches the number line.

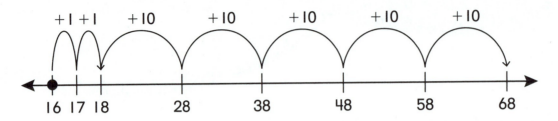

_____ + _____ = _____

9.3 Make a 10 to Add

6. 42 + 6 = _____

Make a 10?   Yes   No

7. 27 + 7 = _____

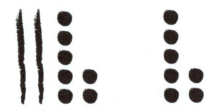

Make a 10?   Yes   No

MP Logic Complete.

8.
34 + 7

34 + ◯ + ◯

40 + ◯

34 + 7 = _____

9.
59 + 8

59 + ◯ + ◯

60 + ◯

59 + 8 = _____

Add Two-Digit Numbers

Make quick sketches to find the sum.

10. 28
    + 33

Tens	Ones

_____ tens _____ one

11. 49
    + 24

Tens	Ones

_____ tens _____ ones

12. **Modeling Real Life** Your club earns a badge for every 10 trees planted. Your club plants 25 trees in the fall and 25 in the spring. How many badges does your club earn?

_____ badges

Chapter 9   four hundred ninety-nine   499

9.5 Practice Addition Strategies

13. 19 + 43 = ____

14. 66 + 28 = ____

 9.6 Problem Solving: Addition

15. Your friend has 59 marbles. You have 23 more than your friend. How many marbles do you have?

____ marbles

16. **Modeling Real Life** You need 50 party hats. You have 24. You buy 16 more. Do you have enough party hats?

Yes   No

10 Measure and Compare Lengths

- Have you ever used a map?
- The red pin shows where you are. Which pin is closest to you? Which pin is farthest from you?

Chapter Learning Target:
Understand length.

Chapter Success Criteria:
- I can identify the lengths of objects.
- I can order objects from longest to shortest.
- I can compare different lengths.
- I can measure the length of objects.

Name _____

10 Vocabulary

Review Words
longer
shorter

Organize It

Use the review words to complete the graphic organizer.

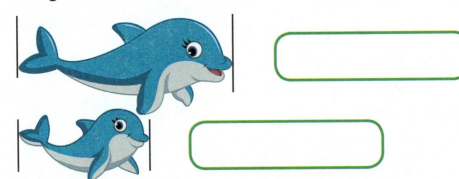

Define It

Use your vocabulary cards to identify the words. Find each word in the word search.

1.

2.

3.

K T L M S R A L E
G E U B H L Q O W
S R O N O K G N F
D C U A R X Y G I
L E N G T H K E V
B A N I E W B S O
J P U R S O E T Y
C A W S T U N K R
L O M E A S U R E

Chapter 10 Vocabulary Cards

length	length unit
longest	measure
shortest	

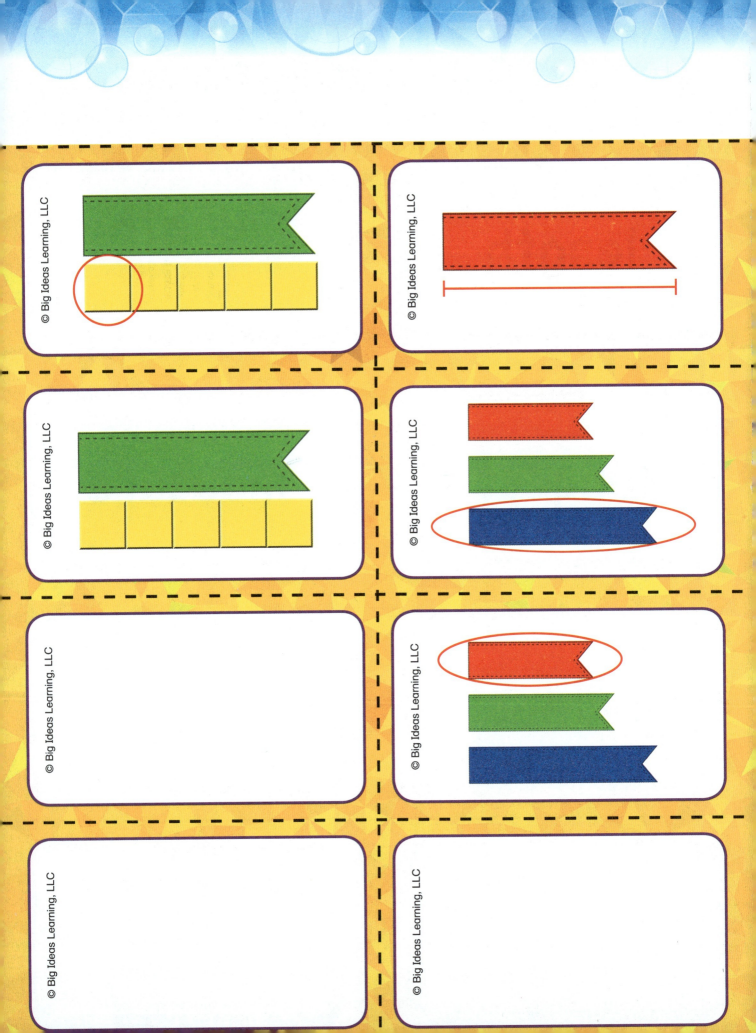

Name _____

Learning Target: Order objects by length.

Order Objects by Length 10.1

Explore and Grow

Draw an object that is shorter than the pencil and longer than the crayon.

Communicate Clearly
Use *longer* in a sentence to describe two objects in your classroom.

Chapter 10 | Lesson 1

five hundred three 503

Think and Grow

Order from longest to shortest.

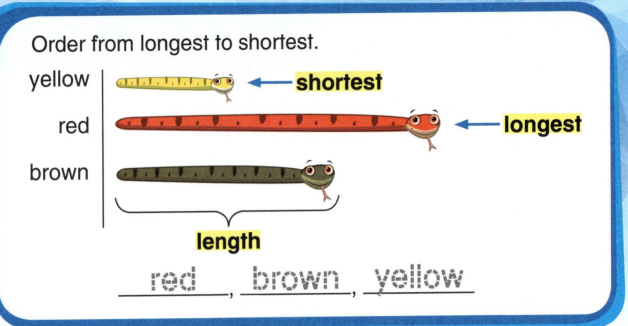

red , _brown_ , _yellow_

Show and Grow I can do it!

1. Order from longest to shortest.

   purple
   blue
   pink

   _____ , _____ , _____

2. Order from shortest to longest.

   green
   yellow
   black

   _____ , _____ , _____

Name _____

 Apply and Grow: Practice

3. Order from longest to shortest.

purple
green
red

_____ , _____ , _____

4. Order from shortest to longest.

green
pink
blue

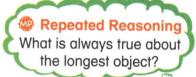
Repeated Reasoning
What is always true about the longest object?

_____ , _____ , _____

5. **YOU BE THE TEACHER** Your friend ordered from shortest to longest. Is your friend correct? Explain.

yellow
red
green

___yellow___ , ___green___ , ___red___

Chapter 10 | Lesson 1

five hundred five 505

Think and Grow: Modeling Real Life

Your yarn is longer than Newton's. Descartes's is longer than Newton's and shorter than yours. Who has the longest yarn?

Draw a picture:

You

Newton

Descartes

Make a Plan
Whose yarn should you draw first?

Who has the longest yarn?

You   Newton   Descartes

Show and Grow   I can think deeper!

6. Descartes's pencil is shorter than Newton's. Yours is shorter than Newton's and longer than Descartes's. Who has the shortest pencil?

Draw a picture:

Descartes

Newton

You

Who has the shortest pencil?

Descartes   Newton   You

Name _____

Practice 10.1

Learning Target: Order objects by length.

Order from longest to shortest.

purple | ────────
green | ──────
pink | ───────

purple, _pink_, _green_

Order from longest to shortest.

1. bat 1 | (medium bat)
   bat 2 | (longest bat)
   bat 3 | (shortest bat)

   _____, _____, _____

2. gold | (longest stroke)
   red | (shortest stroke)
   blue | (medium stroke)

   _____, _____, _____

Chapter 10 | Lesson 1 five hundred seven 507

3. Order from shortest to longest.

vine 1

vine 2

vine 3

_____, _____, _____

4. **Analyze a Problem** Use the clues to match.
The red pencil is longer than the yellow pencil.
The shortest pencil is blue.

blue

red

yellow

5. **Modeling Real Life** Your jump rope is longer than Newton's. Descartes's is longer than Newton's and shorter than yours. Who has the longest jump rope?

Who has the longest jump rope?

You   Newton   Descartes

Review & Refresh

Compare.

6. 25 ◯ 52

7. 41 ◯ 44

Name _____

Learning Target: Compare the lengths of two objects using a third object.

Use string to compare the keys. Which key is longer? How do you know?

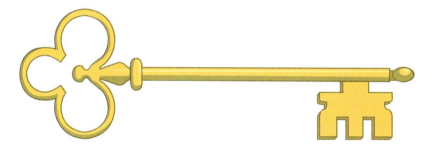

Choose Tools
If you do not have string, what else can you use to compare the lengths of the objects?

Chapter 10 | **Lesson 2**

five hundred nine 509

Think and Grow

Circle the longer object.

Use the string to compare the lengths.

The stick is longer than the string. The string is longer than the frog. So, the stick is longer than the frog.

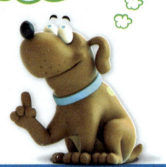

Show and Grow I can do it!

1. Circle the longer object.

2. Draw a line through the shorter object.

Name _____

✓ Apply and Grow: Practice

3. Draw a line through the shorter object.

4. Circle the longer object.

5. **DIG DEEPER!** Which object is longer? Explain.

_____

_____

Chapter 10 | Lesson 2

Think and Grow: Modeling Real Life

A green crayon is shorter than a blue crayon. The blue crayon is shorter than a yellow crayon. Is the green crayon longer than or shorter than the yellow crayon?

Draw a picture: green

blue

yellow

Longer   Shorter

Show and Grow   I can think deeper!

6. A yellow ribbon is longer than a pink ribbon. The pink ribbon is longer than a blue ribbon. Is the yellow ribbon longer than or shorter than the blue ribbon?

Draw a picture: yellow

pink

blue

Longer   Shorter

Name _____

Practice 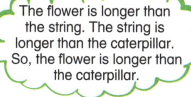 10.2

Learning Target: Compare the lengths of two objects using a third object.

Circle the longer object.

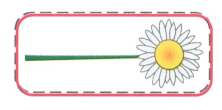  

The flower is longer than the string. The string is longer than the caterpillar. So, the flower is longer than the caterpillar.

1. Circle the longer object.

2. Draw a line through the shorter object.

Chapter 10 | Lesson 2   five hundred thirteen   513

3. **Analyze a Problem** Use the clues to match.
The blue string is longer than the orange string.
The purple string is shorter than the orange string.

blue

orange

purple

4. **Modeling Real Life** A kayak is shorter than a canoe. The canoe is shorter than a paddle board. Is the kayak longer than or shorter than the paddle board?

Longer   Shorter

5. **DIG DEEPER!** A city bus is shorter than a tractor trailer. A van is shorter than a city bus. Compare the tractor trailer and the van.

Review & Refresh

6. Circle the objects that have capacity as an attribute.

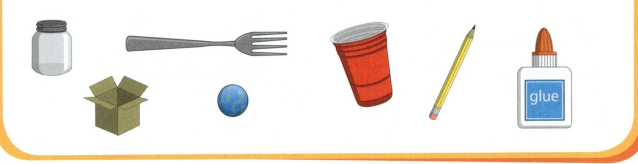

514   five hundred fourteen

Name _____

Measure Lengths

Learning Target: Use like objects to measure length.

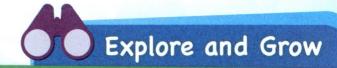

Find and measure the objects shown in your classroom.

Chapter 10 | **Lesson 3** five hundred fifteen **515**

Think and Grow

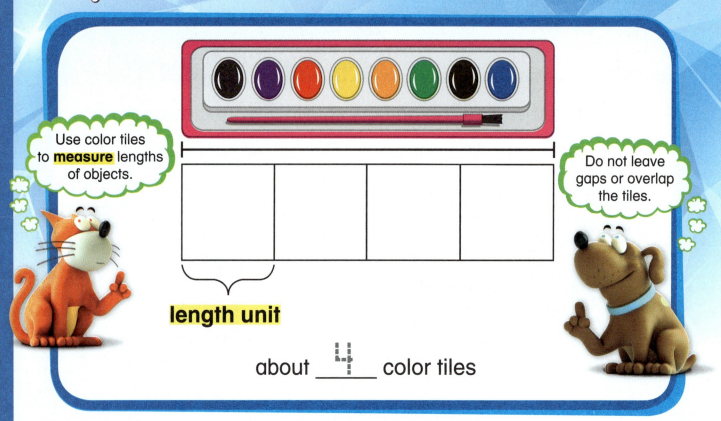

Use color tiles to **measure** lengths of objects.

Do not leave gaps or overlap the tiles.

length unit

about __4__ color tiles

Show and Grow — I can do it!

Measure.

1.

   about _____ color tile

2.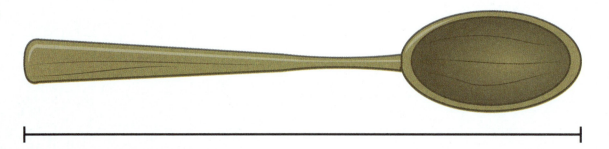

   about _____ color tiles

Name _____

 Apply and Grow: Practice

Measure.

3.

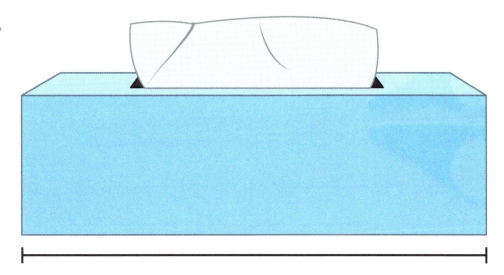

about _____ color tiles

4.

about _____ color tiles

5. **Precision** Which picture shows the correct way to measure the straw?

Chapter 10 | Lesson 3

five hundred seventeen 517

Think and Grow: Modeling Real Life

Will the scissors fit inside a pencil case that is 7 color tiles long?

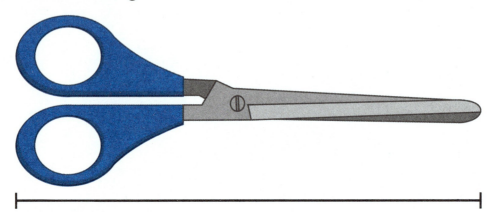

Circle: Yes   No

Tell how you know: _____

Does It Make Sense? To fit inside, should the scissors be shorter or longer than the case?

Show and Grow — I can think deeper!

6. Will the cell phone fit inside a case that is 5 color tiles long?

Circle: Yes   No

Tell how you know: _____

518   five hundred eighteen

Name _____

Practice 10.3

Learning Target: Use like objects to measure length.

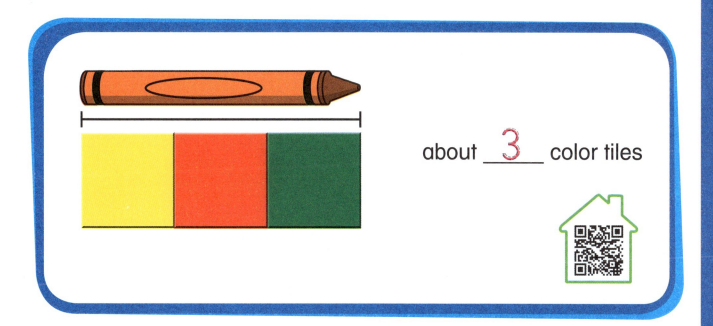

about __3__ color tiles

Measure.

1.

about ____ color tiles

2.

about ____ color tiles

3.

about ____ color tiles

Chapter 10 | Lesson 3

five hundred nineteen 519

4. **Reasoning** The green yarn is about 3 color tiles long. How long is the blue yarn?

about _____ color tiles

5. **Modeling Real Life** Will the gift card fit inside an envelope that is 8 color tiles long?

Circle: Yes   No

Tell how you know:

6. **DIG DEEPER!** Draw a bookmark that is 2 color tiles longer than the gift card in Exercise 5. Will it fit inside the envelope?

Review & Refresh

7. $72 + 19 =$ _____

8. $54 + 9 =$ _____

Name _____

Measure More Lengths 10.4

Learning Target: Measure an object in different ways.

Explore and Grow

Find and measure the objects shown in your classroom two ways. What do you notice?

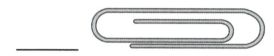

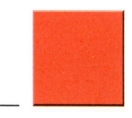

Chapter 10 | Lesson 4

five hundred twenty-one 521

Think and Grow

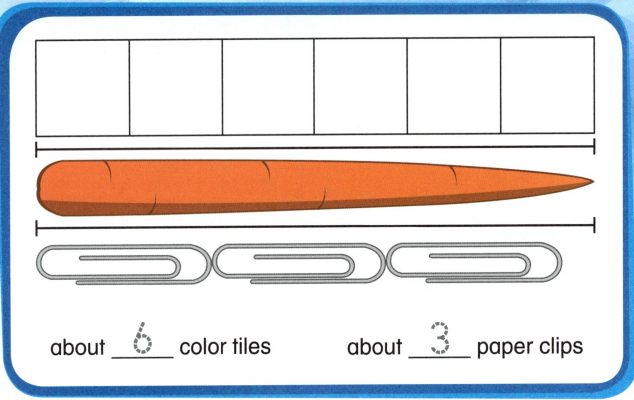

about __6__ color tiles   about __3__ paper clips

Show and Grow — I can do it!

Measure.

1.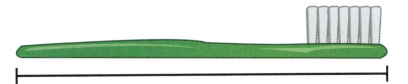

about _____ color tiles   about _____ paper clips

2.

about _____ color tiles   about _____ paper clips

Name _____

 Apply and Grow: Practice

Measure.

3.

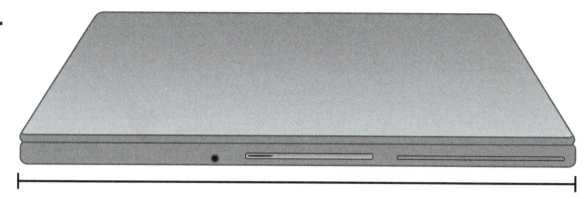

about _____ color tiles   about _____ paper clips

4.

about _____ color tiles   about _____ paper clips

5. **YOU BE THE TEACHER** Your friend says the pencil is more paper clips long than color tiles. Is your friend correct? Explain.

Chapter 10 | Lesson 4   five hundred twenty-three 523

Think and Grow: Modeling Real Life

Your guitar is 33 color tiles long. Is your guitar more than or less than 33 paper clips long?

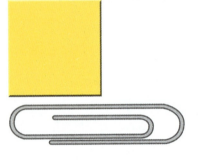   

Circle: more than 33   less than 33

Tell how you know:

Show and Grow I can think deeper!

6. Your mailbox is 11 paper clips long. Is your mailbox more than or less than 11 color tiles long?

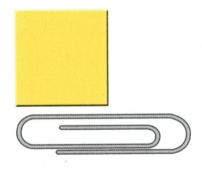   

Circle: more than 11   less than 11

Tell how you know:

Name _____

Practice

Learning Target: Measure an object in different ways.

about __2__ color tiles

about __1__ paper clip

Measure.

1.

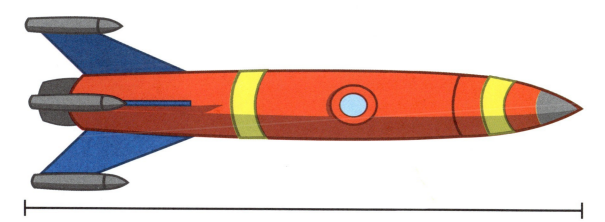

about ____ color tiles   about ____ paper clips

Chapter 10 | Lesson 4

2. **YOU BE THE TEACHER** Your friend says the marker is more color tiles long than paper clips. Is your friend correct? Explain.

3. **Modeling Real Life** Your folder is 15 color tiles long. Is your folder more than or less than 15 paper clips long?

Circle: more than 15   less than 15

Tell how you know:

4. **DIG DEEPER!** Your crayon is 4 color tiles long. About how many paper clips long is the crayon? Explain.

about _____ paper clips

Review & Refresh

5. 8 tigers swim.
5 tigers leave.
How many tigers are left?

_____ − _____ = _____

_____ tigers

Name _____

Solve *Compare* Problems Involving Length

10.5

Learning Target: Solve *compare* word problems involving length.

Explore and Grow

Draw a line that is 2 color tiles longer than the pencil.

Draw a line that is 2 color tiles shorter than the pencil.

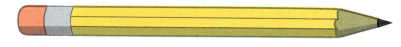

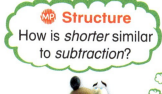

Structure
How is *shorter* similar to *subtraction*?

Chapter 10 | Lesson 5

five hundred twenty-seven 527

Think and Grow

Your shoe is 7 color tiles long. Your friend's is 9 color tiles long. How many tiles shorter is your shoe?

Friend: 9
You: 7 2

9 − 7 = 2

7 + 2 = 9

____2____ color tiles

Show and Grow I can do it!

1. Your lunch box is 6 paper clips long. Your friend's is 3 paper clips long. How many paper clips longer is your lunch box?

You:
Friend:

___ − ___ = ___

___ + ___ = ___

_____ paper clips

Name _____

  Apply and Grow: Practice

2. Your scarf is 10 paper clips long. Your friend's is 7 paper clips long. How many paper clips longer is your scarf?

You:

Friend:

____ − ____ = ____

____ + ____ = ____

____ paper clips

3. Your marker is 6 color tiles long. Your friend's is 7 color tiles long. How many tiles shorter is your marker?

Friend:

You:

____ ◯ ____ = ____

____ color tile

4. **Reasoning** Your pencil is 4 color tiles long. Your friend's is 2 color tiles long. Complete the sentences.

Your pencil is _____ color tiles _____ than your friend's.

Your friend's pencil is _____ color tiles _____ than yours.

Chapter 10 | Lesson 5   five hundred twenty-nine   **529**

Think and Grow: Modeling Real Life

Your friend's paper chain is 6 paper clips shorter than yours. Your chain is 12 paper clips long. How long is your friend's?

Model: You: [   ]
         Friend: [   ][   ]

Equation:

_____ paper clips long

Show and Grow I can think deeper!

5. Your paper airplane is 9 color tiles shorter than your friend's. Your friend's paper airplane is 16 color tiles long. How long is yours?

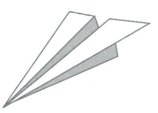

Model: Friend: [   ]
         You: [   ][   ]

Equation:

_____ color tiles long

Name _____

Practice 10.5

Learning Target: Solve *compare* word problems involving length.

Your book is 4 color tiles long. Your friend's is 6 color tiles long. How many tiles shorter is your book?

Friend: | 6 |
You: | 4 | 2 |

6 − 4 = 2

4 + 2 = 6

____2____ color tiles

1. Your backpack is 15 paper clips long. Your friend's is 12 paper clips long. How many paper clips longer is your backpack?

You:
Friend:

___ − ___ = ___

___ + ___ = ___

_____ paper clips

Chapter 10 | Lesson 5 — five hundred thirty-one

2. **Reasoning** Your baseball mitt is 8 paper clips long. Your friend's is 7 paper clips long. Complete the sentences.

   Your friend's baseball mitt is _____ paper clip _____ than yours.

   Your baseball mitt is _____ paper clip _____ than your friend's.

3. **Modeling Real Life** Your desk is 7 paper clips longer than your friend's. Your friend's desk is 14 paper clips long. How long is yours?

   You:
   Friend:

   _____ paper clips long

4. **DIG DEEPER!** In Exercise 3, your cousin's desk is longer than your friend's desk, but shorter than your desk. What is the greatest length that your cousin's desk could be? the shortest?

   Review & Refresh

   5. 5 + 5 = _____
   6. 2 + 2 = _____

Name _____

Performance Task 10

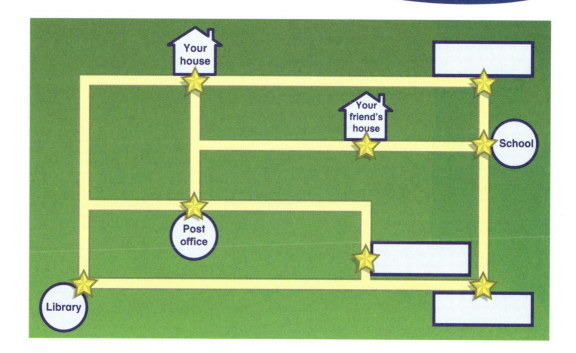

1. Use a piece of string to compare the routes from your house to the library, the post office, and the school. Order the routes from shortest to longest.

   _____, _____, _____

2. Use a piece of string to measure the different routes from your house to your friend's house. Color the route you would use to ride your bike to your friend's house.

3. a. The bakery is farther from your house than the pool. The park is closer to your house than the pool. Which place is closest to your house?

   Park   Bakery   Pool

   b. Label the park, bakery, and pool on the map.

Chapter 10   five hundred thirty-three   533

Fish Measurement

To Play: Flip over 3 Fish Measurement Cards. Compare the lengths of the 3 fish. Place each card in the correct box. Discuss your answers with your partner.

Shortest

Longest

Name _____

Chapter Practice 10

10.1 Order Objects by Length

1. Order from longest to shortest.

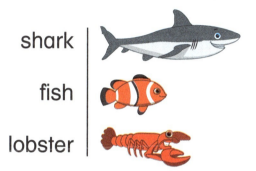

shark

fish

lobster

_____, _____, _____

2. **Analyze a Problem** A green snake is shorter than a black snake. A brown snake is shorter than the black snake. Which snake is the longest?

    green   black   brown

10.2 Compare Lengths Indirectly

3. Circle the longer object.

Chapter 10   five hundred thirty-five   535

4. Circle the longer object.

5. Draw a line through the shorter object.

10.3 Measure Lengths

Measure.

6.

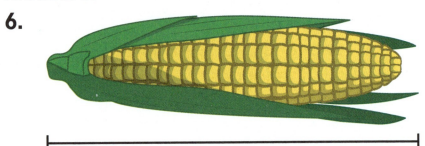

about _____ color tiles

7.

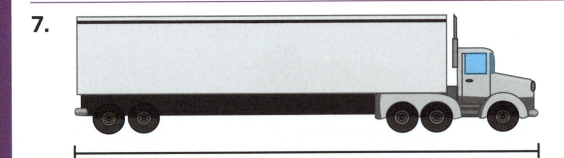

about _____ color tiles

10.4 Measure More Lengths

Measure.

8.

about _____ color tiles   about _____ paper clips

9. **Modeling Real Life** Your hockey stick is 18 paper clips long. Is your hockey stick more than or less than 18 color tiles long?

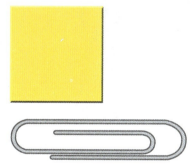

Circle: more than 18   less than 18

Tell how you know:

10.5 Solve *Compare* Problems Involving Length

10. Your water bottle is 5 paper clips long. Your friend's is 4 paper clips long. How many paper clips longer is your water bottle?

You:
Friend:

____ − ____ = ____

____ + ____ = ____

____ paper clip

11. Your bookshelf is 19 color tiles long. Your friend's is 15 color tiles long. How many tiles longer is your bookshelf?

You:
Friend:

____ ◯ ____ = ____

____ color tiles

12. **MP Reasoning** Your pencil is 6 color tiles long. Your friend's is 3 color tiles long. Complete the sentences.

Your pencil is ____ color tiles _____ than your friend's.

Your friend's pencil is ____ color tiles _____ than yours.

11 Represent and Interpret Data

- What color are your eyes?
- Do any of your friends or family members have the same color eyes as you?

Chapter Learning Target:
Understand data.

Chapter Success Criteria:
- I can record data on a tally chart.
- I can use a tally chart.
- I can compare data.
- I can interpret data.

Vocabulary

Review Words
category
mark

Organize It

Use the review words to complete the graphic organizer.

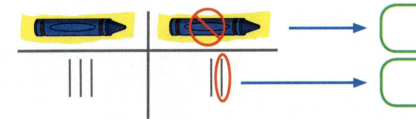

Define It

Use your vocabulary cards to match.

1. bar graph

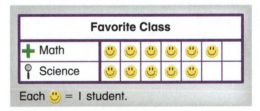

2. picture graph

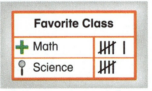

3. tally chart

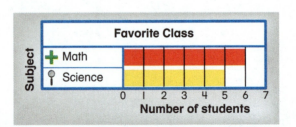

Chapter 11 Vocabulary Cards

bar graph	data
picture graph	tally chart
tally mark	

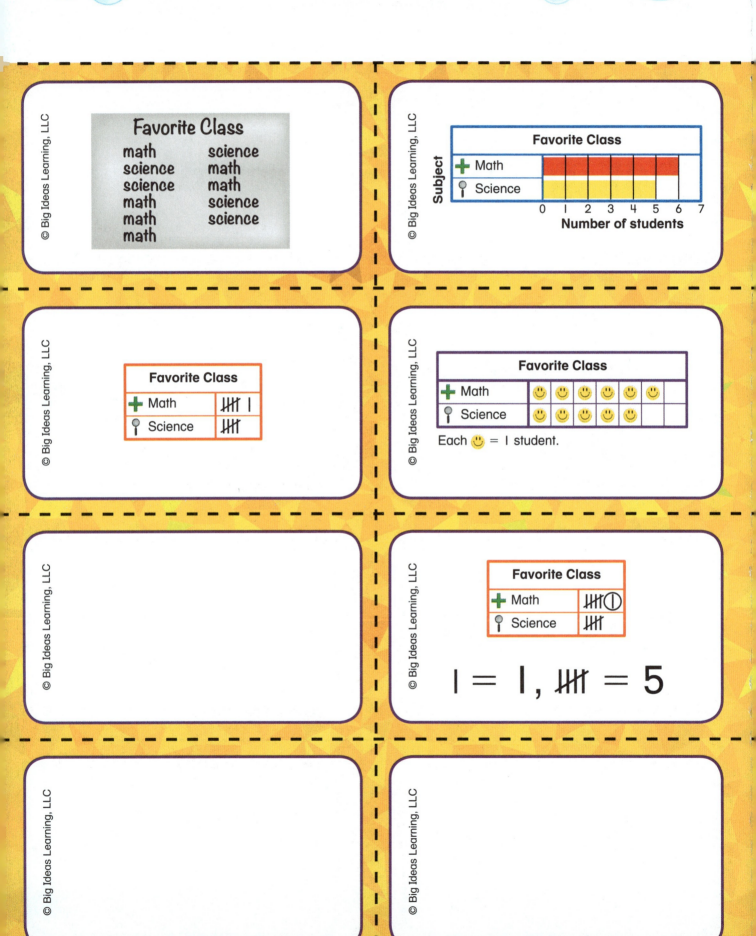

Name _____

Learning Target: Make a tally chart to organize and understand data.

Sort and Organize Data

Explore and Grow

Explain how you can sort the objects.

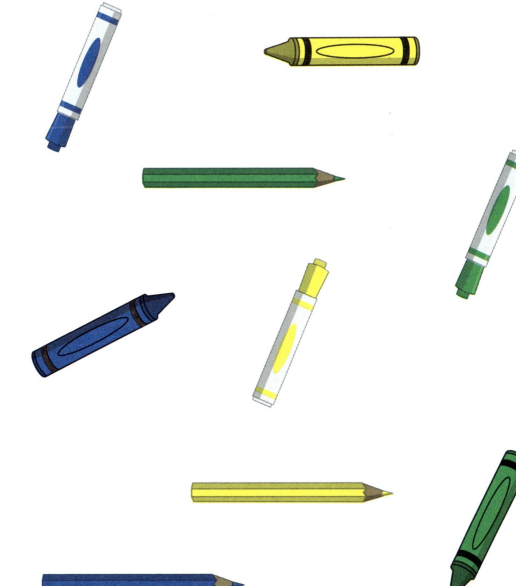

Chapter 11 | Lesson 1

five hundred forty-one 541

Think and Grow

You can organize **data** in a tally chart.

tally chart

Medals	
🏅 Gold	~~||||~~ |||
🥈 Silver	||||
🥉 Bronze	|||

tally mark

Structure
Each | means 1.
Each ~~||||~~ means 5.
Why would you use ~~||||~~ for 5 instead of |||||?

Show and Grow — I can do it!

1. Complete the tally chart.

Stickers	
☂ Umbrella	
🪣 Bucket	
🦀 Crab	

Apply and Grow: Practice

2. Complete the tally chart.

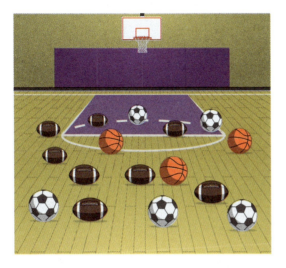

Balls	
Football	
Soccer ball	
Basketball	

3. **Reasoning** Which sentences are correct?

Stuffed Animals	
Tiger	|||| ||||
Fox	|||| ||
Raccoon	|||| ||

There are 7 tigers.

There are 7 foxes.

The numbers of foxes and raccoons are the same.

There are 3 raccoons.

Think and Grow: Modeling Real Life

Weather	
☀ Sunny	⊞ III
☁ Cloudy	IIII
🌧 Rainy	III

How many sunny days are there? _____ days

Is the number of cloudy days greater than or less than the number of rainy days?

greater than   less than

Repeated Reasoning
Do you need to count the tally marks to compare? Explain.

Show and Grow   I can think deeper!

4.

Flowers in a Garden	
🌹 Rose	⊞ I
🌻 Sunflower	II
🌼 Daisy	⊞ II

How many sunflowers are there? _____ sunflowers

Is the number of roses greater than or less than the number of daisies?

greater than   less than

Name _____

Practice 11.1

Learning Target: Make a tally chart to organize and understand data.

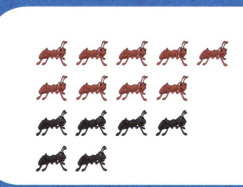

Ants	
Red	𝍷𝍷𝍷𝍷𝍷 𝍷𝍷𝍷𝍷
Black	𝍷𝍷𝍷𝍷𝍷 𝍷

1. Complete the tally chart.

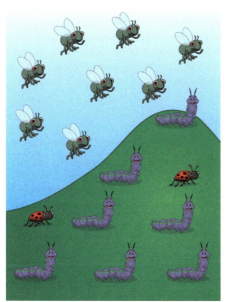

Insects	
Caterpillar	
Fly	
Ladybug	

2. **Reasoning** Which sentences are correct?

Favorite Movie	
Superhero	𝍷𝍷𝍷𝍷𝍷
Princess	𝍷𝍷𝍷𝍷𝍷 𝍷𝍷𝍷𝍷
Mystery	𝍷𝍷𝍷𝍷𝍷

9 students like princess movies.

4 students like superhero movies.

Princess movies are the most favorite.

Chapter 11 | Lesson 1   five hundred forty-five   545

3. **Modeling Real Life** Use the tally chart.

Favorite Breakfast		
	Yogurt				
	Fruit	||||
	Cereal	||||	

How many students chose fruit? _____ students

Is the number of students who chose yogurt greater than or less than the number of students who chose cereal?

        greater than   less than

---

4. **DIG DEEPER!** Complete the tally chart.

There are more 🟣 than 🟨.

There are fewer 🟨 than 🔺.

There are fewer 🔺 than 🟣.

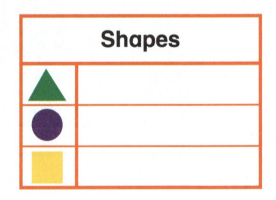

Review & Refresh

Compare.

5. 45 ◯ 55   6. 74 ◯ 47   7. 22 ◯ 22

Name _____

Learning Target: Understand the data shown by a picture graph.

Explore and Grow

How are the graphs similar? How are they different?

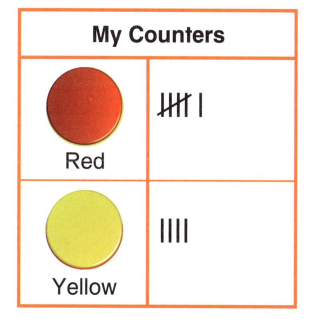

Each ◯ = 1 counter.

Chapter 11 | Lesson 2   five hundred forty-seven   547

Think and Grow

picture graph

Favorite Fruit

🍌 Banana	🙂	🙂	🙂					
🍎 Apple	🙂	🙂	🙂	🙂	🙂	🙂	🙂	
🍊 Orange	🙂	🙂	🙂	🙂	🙂			

Each 🙂 = 1 student.

How many students chose banana? __3__

Which fruit is the most favorite?

Show and Grow — I can do it!

1.

Favorite School Trip

🦖 Museum	🙂	🙂	🙂	🙂	🙂	🙂	🙂	🙂
🐅 Zoo	🙂	🙂	🙂	🙂	🙂	🙂		
👸 Play	🙂	🙂						

Each 🙂 = 1 student.

How many students chose museum? _____

Which trip is the least favorite?

Apply and Grow: Practice

2.

Favorite Lunch									
Pasta	😊	😊	😊	😊	😊				
Soup	😊	😊	😊						
Taco	😊	😊	😊	😊	😊	😊	😊	😊	

Each 😊 = 1 student.

How many students chose pasta? _____

How many students chose soup? _____

Which lunch is the least favorite?

3. **Communicate Clearly** In Exercise 2, how do you know which lunch is the most favorite?

_____

_____

_____

Chapter 11 | Lesson 2

Think and Grow: Modeling Real Life

Favorite Activity at the Fair

🎡 Rides	🙂	🙂	🙂	🙂	🙂		
🐑 Animals	🙂	🙂					
🎪 Games	🙂	🙂	🙂	🙂			

Each 🙂 = 1 student.

Is the number of students who chose rides greater than, less than, or equal to the number of students who chose animals?

greater than   less than   equal to

Show and Grow   I can think deeper!

4.

Favorite Forest Animal

🐸 Frog	🙂	🙂	🙂			
🐻 Bear	🙂	🙂	🙂	🙂	🙂	🙂
🦊 Fox	🙂	🙂	🙂			

Each 🙂 = 1 student.

Is the number of students who chose frog greater than, less than, or equal to the number of students who chose bear?

greater than   less than   equal to

Name _____

Practice 11.2

Learning Target: Understand the data shown by a picture graph.

Favorite Snack

🥨	Pretzels	🙂	🙂	🙂	🙂	🙂	🙂
🍎	Apple	🙂	🙂	🙂			

Each 🙂 = 1 student.

Which snack is the most favorite?

1.

Favorite Season

💮	Spring	🙂	🙂	🙂					
☀️	Summer	🙂	🙂	🙂	🙂	🙂	🙂	🙂	
🍁	Fall	🙂	🙂	🙂	🙂				
❄️	Winter	🙂							

Each 🙂 = 1 student.

How many students chose summer? _____

How many students chose fall? _____

Which season is the least favorite?

Chapter 11 | Lesson 2

five hundred fifty-one 551

2. **Communicate Clearly** How do you know which category has the least when looking at a picture graph?

   _____

3. **Modeling Real Life** Use the picture graph.

   Favorite Drink at Lunch

Milk	🙂	🙂	🙂					
Water	🙂	🙂	🙂	🙂				
Juice	🙂	🙂	🙂	🙂				

   Each 🙂 = 1 student.

   Is the number of students who chose water greater than, less than, or equal to the number of students who chose juice?

   greater than   less than   equal to

4. **DIG DEEPER!** In Exercise 3, four more students choose their favorite drink. Is it possible for the picture graph to show the same number of students in each category? Explain.

   Yes   No   _____

   Review & Refresh

   5. 31 + 40 = _____   6. 62 + 20 = _____

Name _____

Learning Target: Understand the data shown by a bar graph.

Read and Interpret Bar Graphs
11.3

Explore and Grow

How are the graphs similar? How are they different?

Favorite Fruit					
🫐 Blueberries	😊	😊	😊		
🍎 Apple	😊	😊	😊	😊	
🍇 Grapes	😊				

Each 😊 = 1 student.

Chapter 11 | Lesson 3

five hundred fifty-three 553

Think and Grow

bar graph

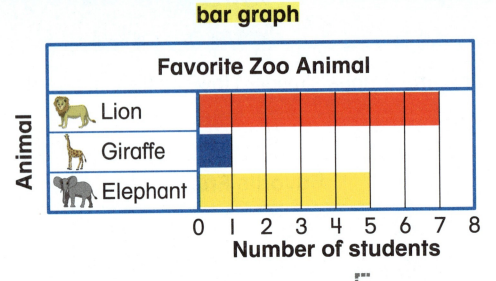

How many students chose elephant? __5__

Which animal is the most favorite?

Show and Grow I can do it!

1.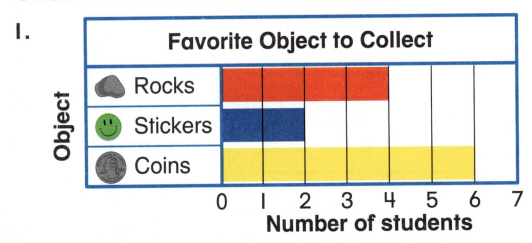

How many students chose coins? _____

Which object is the least favorite?

Apply and Grow: Practice

2.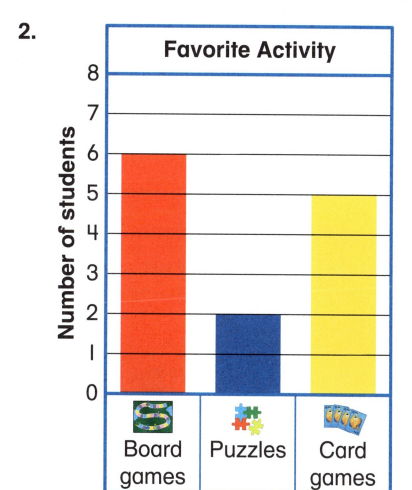

How many students chose card games?

_____

How many students chose board games?

_____

Which activity is the most favorite?

3. **DIG DEEPER!** Order the activities in Exercise 2 from the most favorite to the least favorite.

_____ , _____ , _____

Think and Grow: Modeling Real Life

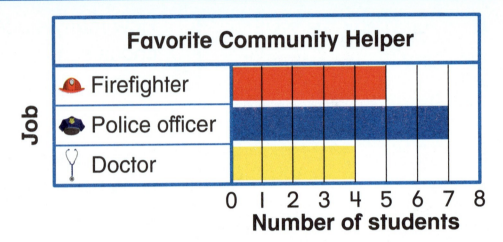

Is the number of students who chose firefighter greater than, less than, or equal to the number of students who chose doctor?

greater than   less than   equal to

Show and Grow   I can think deeper!

4.

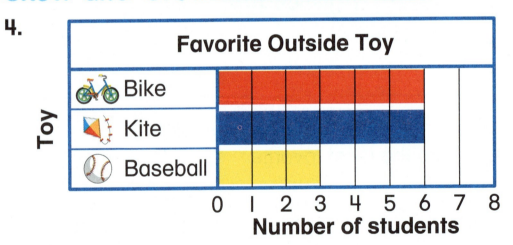

Is the number of students who chose bike greater than, less than, or equal to the number of students who chose kite?

greater than   less than   equal to

Name _____

Practice 11.3

Learning Target: Understand the data shown by a bar graph.

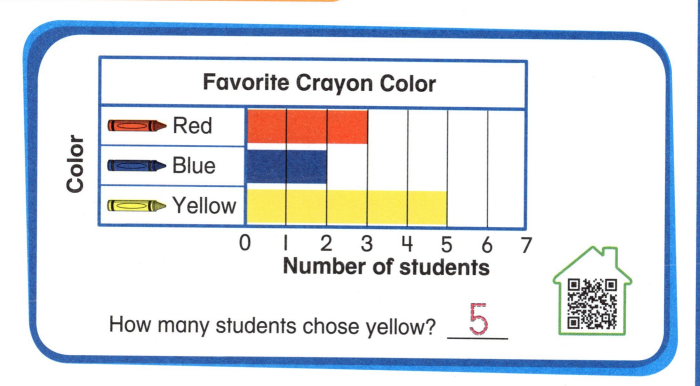

How many students chose yellow? __5__

1.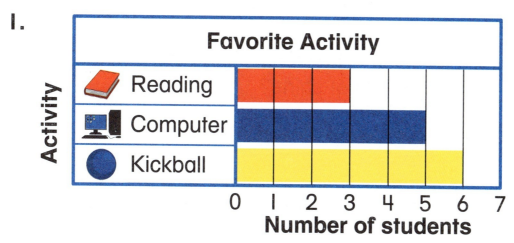

How many students chose reading? ____

How many students chose kickball? ____

Which activity is the least favorite?

Chapter 11 | Lesson 3

five hundred fifty-seven 557

2. **Communicate Clearly** How do you know which category has the most when looking at a bar graph?

   _____

   _____

3. **Modeling Real Life** Use the bar graph.

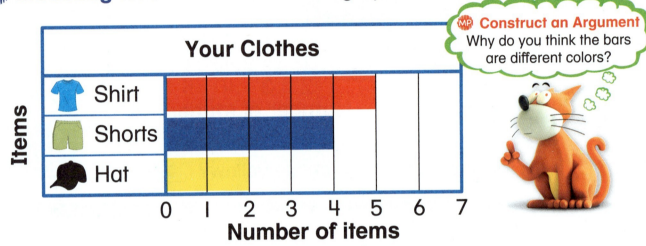

   Construct an Argument Why do you think the bars are different colors?

   Is the number of pairs of shorts greater than, less than, or equal to the number of shirts?

   greater than   less than   equal to

4. **DIG DEEPER!** In Exercise 3, how many more shirts do you have than hats?

   _____ shirts

Review & Refresh

5. $9 + 1 + 7 =$ _____

6. $6 + 3 + 6 =$ _____

Name _____

Learning Target: Make picture graphs and bar graphs.

Represent Data 11.4

Explore and Grow

Use your color tiles to complete the tally chart and the picture graph.

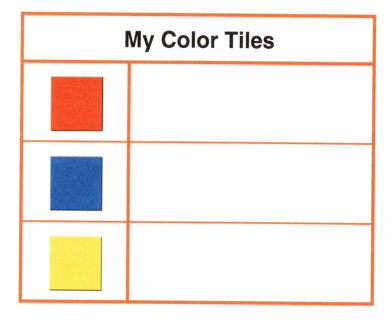

Each ◯ = 1 color tile.

Chapter 11 | Lesson 4

five hundred fifty-nine 559

Think and Grow

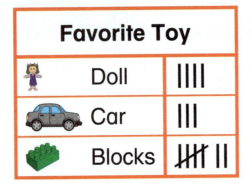

Each 🙂 = 1 student.

Show and Grow — I can do it!

1. Complete the bar graph.

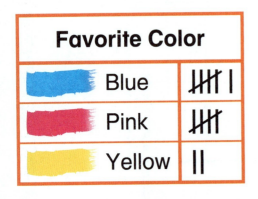

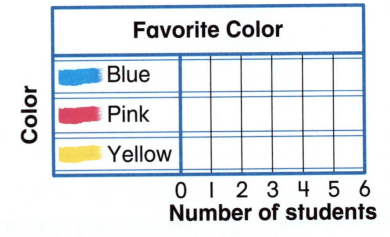

Apply and Grow: Practice

2. Complete the picture graph.

Favorite Farm Animal

Pig	IIII
Cow	IIII I
Horse	IIII

Favorite Farm Animal

Pig						
Cow						
Horse						

Each 🙂 = 1 student.

3. Complete the bar graph.

Favorite Sport

Swimming	IIII
Karate	II
Soccer	IIII

Favorite Sport

Sport: Swimming, Karate, Soccer

0 1 2 3 4 5 6 7
Number of students

Chapter 11 | Lesson 4   five hundred sixty-one

Think and Grow: Modeling Real Life

You ask 10 students whether they are right-handed or left-handed. 2 are left-handed. The rest are right-handed. Complete the picture graph.

How We Write									
✋ Right-handed									
✋ Left-handed	🙂	🙂							

Each 🙂 = 1 student.

Show and Grow — I can think deeper!

4. You ask 11 students whether they like the swings or the slide. 5 like the swings. The rest like the slide. Complete the bar graph.

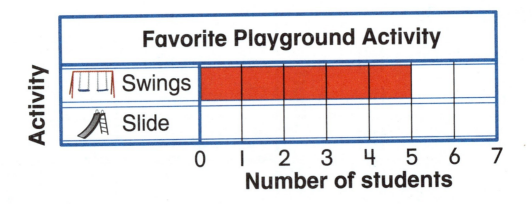

562 five hundred sixty-two

Name _____

Practice

Learning Target: Make picture graphs and bar graphs.

Favorite Socks

🧦	Black	|||||
🧦	Red		
🧦	Stripes	|||||

Favorite Socks

🧦	Black	🙂	🙂	🙂	🙂	🙂	
🧦	Red	🙂					
🧦	Stripes	🙂	🙂	🙂	🙂	🙂	

Each 🙂 = 1 student.

1. Complete the bar graph.

Favorite Winter Activity

🥏	Sledding	|||||	
⛸	Skating	|||
☃	Snowman	||||

Favorite Winter Activity

Activity		0	1	2	3	4	5	6	7
	Sledding								
	Skating								
	Snowman								

Number of students

Choose Tools
What tools can you use to represent the bars in the bar graph?

Chapter 11 | Lesson 4   five hundred sixty-three   563

2. Complete the picture graph.

Balloons	
Blue	llll l
Red	ll

Balloons						
Blue						
Red						

Each ◯ = 1 balloon.

3. **DIG DEEPER!** In a picture graph, each 🙂 represents 5. How can you find the total number of students the picture graph represents?

_____

_____

_____

4. **Modeling Real Life** You ask 8 students whether they buy or pack their lunches. 6 students buy. The rest pack. Complete the picture graph.

Lunch Choices							
Buy	🙂	🙂	🙂	🙂	🙂	🙂	
Pack							

Each 🙂 = 1 student.

Review & Refresh

Find the sum. Then change the order of the addends. Write the new equation.

5. 2 + 6 = ____   ____ + ____ = ____

Name _____

Learning Target: Use data from graphs to answer questions.

Solve Problems Involving Data

Explore and Grow

Complete the bar graph to show 19 toys in all.

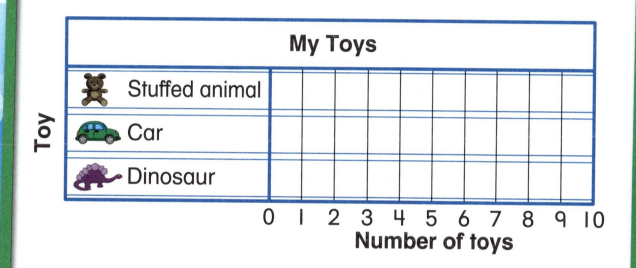

Write a question about your graph. Have your partner answer the question.

MP Find Entry Points
Name something that is true about your bar graph. Use that to help you write your question.

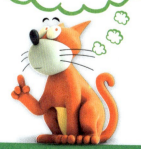

Chapter 11 | Lesson 5

five hundred sixty-five

Think and Grow

How You Get to School	
🚌 Bus	||||| |||||
🚶 Walk		
🚗 Car	|||

How many more students ride a bus than walk?

__10__ ⊖ __1__ = __9__   __9__ students

How many students were asked?

__10__ + __1__ + __3__ = __14__   __14__ students

Show and Grow   I can do it!

1.

Favorite Animal That Flies								
🐦 Bird	😊	😊	😊	😊	😊	😊	
🦇 Bat	😊	😊	😊	😊			
🦋 Butterfly	😊	😊	😊	😊	😊	😊	😊

Each 😊 = 1 student.

How many more students like butterflies than birds?

_____ students

How many students were asked?   _____ students

✓ Apply and Grow: Practice

2.

Favorite Shape

🟧 Square	🙂	🙂	🙂	🙂	🙂	🙂	🙂	
🔴 Circle	🙂	🙂	🙂	🙂	🙂			
🔺 Triangle	🙂	🙂	🙂	🙂	🙂	🙂	🙂	

Each 🙂 = 1 student.

How many fewer students chose circle than square?

_____ fewer students

How many students chose square or triangle?

_____ students

3. **DIG DEEPER!** You ask 9 students to name their favorite rainy-day activity. Complete the bar graph to show how many chose reading. Think: How do you know?

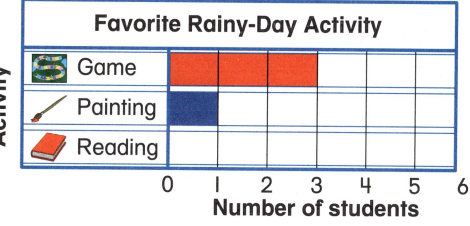

Chapter 11 | Lesson 5

Think and Grow: Modeling Real Life

Write and answer a question using the bar graph.

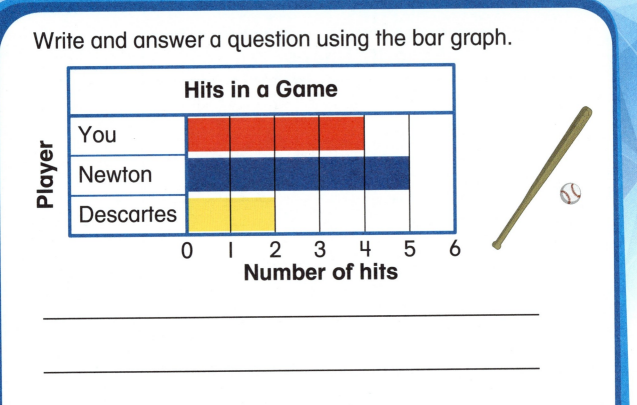

Show and Grow — I can think deeper!

4. Write and answer a question using the tally chart.

Laps Run	
You	||
Descartes	|||||
Newton		

Name _____

Practice 11.5

Learning Target: Use data from graphs to answer questions.

My Writing Tools

	Marker	○	○	○	○		
	Pencil	○	○	○	○	○	

Each ○ = 1 writing tool.

How many writing tools do you have?

__4__ + __5__ = __9__   __9__ writing tools

1. **Stuffed Animals**

   Bear, Penguin, Dog
   Number of stuffed animals: 0 1 2 3 4 5 6 7 8

   How many more dogs are there than penguins?

   _____ more dogs

   How many bears and dogs are there in all?

   _____ bears and dogs

2. **DIG DEEPER!** You ask 19 students to name their favorite fruit. Complete the tally chart to show how many chose apples. Explain how you know.

Favorite Fruit	
Apple	
Banana	||||| ||
Orange	||

_____

_____

_____

3. **Modeling Real Life** Write and answer a question using the bar graph.

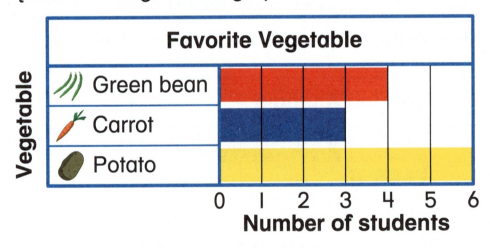

_____

_____

_____

Review & Refresh

4. 51 + 40 = _____

5. 76 + 3 = _____

Name _____

Performance Task 11

1. **Graph Data** Ask your classmates about their eye colors. Use your data to complete the tally chart.

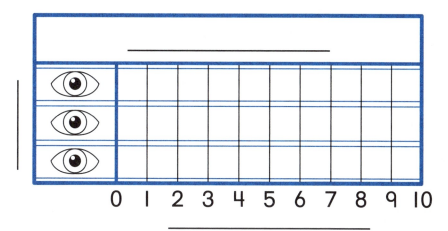

2. Use your tally chart to complete the bar graph.

3. Describe two ways to tell how many students you asked.

   _____
   _____

4. Write and answer a question about your graphs.

   _____
   _____

Chapter 11　　　　　　　　　　　　　　　five hundred seventy-one　571

Spin and Graph

To Play: Spin 10 times. Complete the tally chart. Then complete the bar graph. Answer the Spin and Graph Questions about your graph.

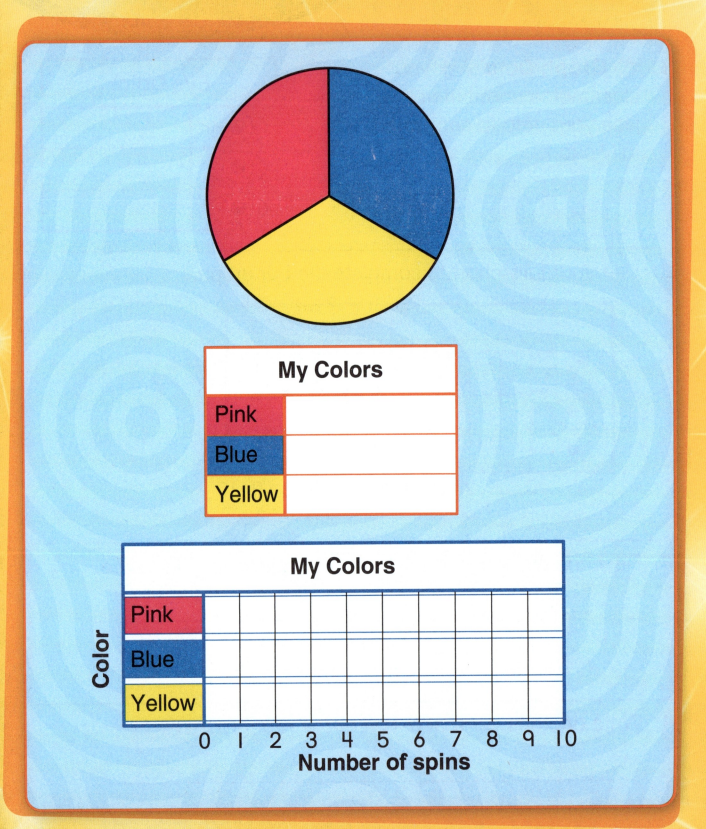

Name _____

Chapter Practice 11

11.1 Sort and Organize Data

Complete the tally chart.

1.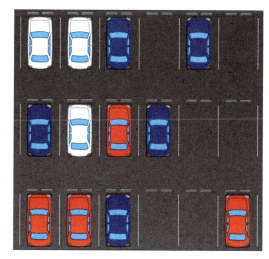

Cars	
🚗 Red	
🚙 White	
🚙 Blue	

2.

Pets	
🐱 Cat	
🐶 Dog	
🐟 Fish	

Chapter 11   five hundred seventy-three   573

11.2 Read and Interpret Picture Graphs

3.

Favorite School Subject							
Art	🙂	🙂	🙂	🙂	🙂		
Math	🙂	🙂	🙂	🙂	🙂	🙂	
Science	🙂	🙂	🙂	🙂			

Each 🙂 = 1 student.

How many students chose science? _____

Which subject is the least favorite?

11.3 Read and Interpret Bar Graphs

4.

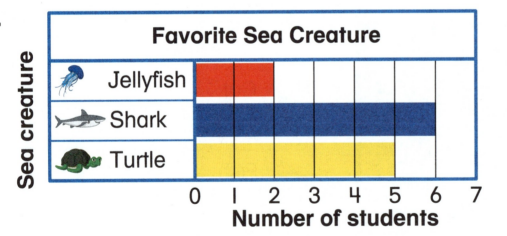

How many students chose turtle? _____

Which is the most favorite sea creature?

11.4 Represent Data

5. Complete the bar graph.

Beads	
Blue	|||||
Red	||
Yellow	||||

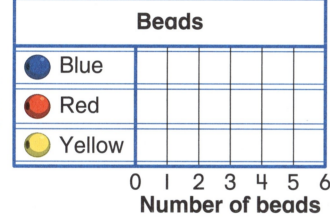

---

6. **Modeling Real Life** You ask 13 students whether they like volleyball or basketball. 7 like volleyball. The rest like basketball. Complete the picture graph.

Favorite Sport								
Volleyball	🙂	🙂	🙂	🙂	🙂	🙂	🙂	
Basketball								

Each 🙂 = 1 student.

Chapter 11   five hundred seventy-five   575

11.5 Solve Problems Involving Data

7.

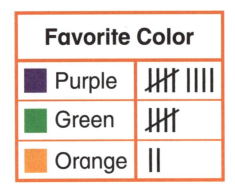

How many fewer students chose green than purple?

_____ fewer students

How many students were asked?

_____ students

---

8. **Modeling Real Life** Write and answer a question using the bar graph.

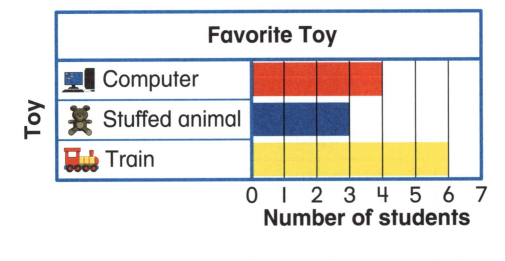

_____

_____

Cumulative Practice 1-11

1. Match each number on the left with a number that is 10 more.

110	102
92	22
40	120
12	50

2. Complete.

$$56 + 6$$

$$56 + \bigcirc + \bigcirc$$

$$60 + \bigcirc$$

$$56 + 6 = \underline{}$$

3. Order from shortest to longest.

blue
yellow
red

_____ , _____ , _____

4. Shade the circle next to the number that tells how many horns there are.

○ 3   ○ 10

○ 6   ○ 19

---

5. Shade the circle next to the sum.

12 + 5 = _____

○ 15   ○ 17

○ 16   ○ 7

---

6. There are 85 pages in a book. You read 10 of them. How many pages are left?

○ 95   ○ 85

○ 75   ○ 80

7. Is each sentence true?

52 is greater than 36.	Yes	No
100 < 90	Yes	No
75 is less than 57.	Yes	No
89 > 81	Yes	No

8. You collect 22 cans for a food drive. Your friend collects 36. How many cans do you and your friend collect in all?

_____ cans

9. Measure.

about _____ color tiles

10. Shade the circles next to the choices that match the model.

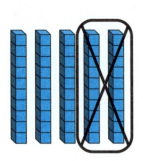

◯ 50 − 30

◯ 5 tens − 2 tens

◯ 50 − 20

◯ 3 tens − 2 tens

11.

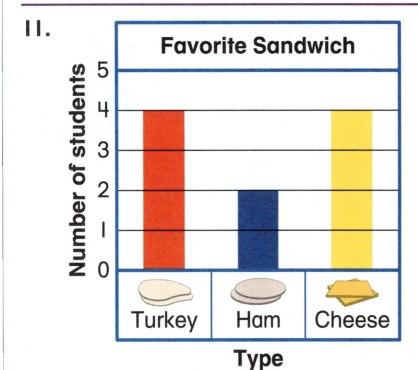

How many students chose ham? _____

Which sandwich is the least favorite?

12. Use each card once to write an addition equation.

____ + ____ = ____

12 Tell Time

- Have you ever been on a field trip?
- Where would you like to go? How long does it take to get there?

Chapter Learning Target:
Understand time.

Chapter Success Criteria:
- I can identify numbers on a clock.
- I can explain how to tell time to the hour.
- I can compare different times on the clock.
- I can draw to show the time.

12 Vocabulary

Organize It

Review Words
above
below
next to

Use the review words to complete the graphic organizer.

Define It

Use your vocabulary cards to identify the word.

1.

2.

3.

4.

Chapter 12 Vocabulary Cards

analog clock	digital clock
half hour	half past
hour	hour hand
minute	minute hand

half past 3

A half hour is 30 minutes.

An hour is 60 minutes.

60 minutes is 1 hour.

Chapter 12 Vocabulary Cards

o'clock

3 o'clock

Name _____

Tell Time to the Hour
12.1

Learning Target: Use the hour hand to tell time to the hour.

 **Explore and Grow**

Write the missing numbers.

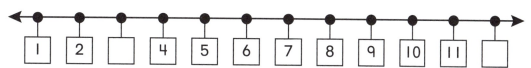

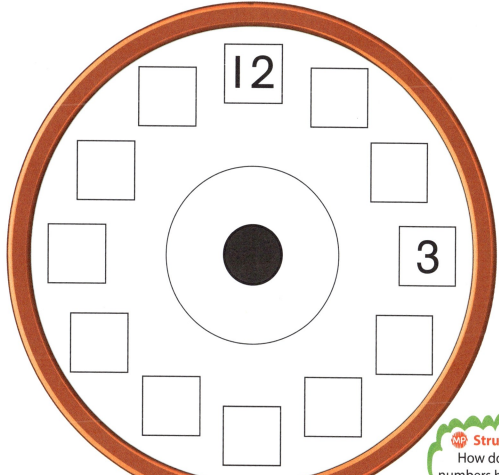

MP Structure
How do the numbers help you know which way the clock hands move?

Chapter 12 | Lesson 1   five hundred eighty-three   583

Think and Grow

analog clock

An **hour** passes when the **hour hand** moves from one number to the next.

It is __2__ **o'clock**.

Show and Grow — I can do it!

Write the time shown by the hour hand.

1.

   _____ o'clock

2.

   _____ o'clock

3.

   _____ o'clock

4.

   _____ o'clock

5.

   _____ o'clock

6.

   _____ o'clock

Name _____

 Apply and Grow: Practice

Write the time shown by the hour hand.

7.

_____ o'clock

8.

_____ o'clock

9.

_____ o'clock

Draw the hour hand to show the time.

10. 5 o'clock

11. 10 o'clock

12. 2 o'clock

13. **Precision** You wake up at 7 o'clock. Which clock shows the time you wake up?

Chapter 12 | Lesson 1

Think and Grow: Modeling Real Life

You eat dinner 1 hour later than your friend. Show and write the time you eat dinner.

Friend   You

_____ o'clock

Show and Grow I can think deeper!

14. Math class starts 1 hour earlier than science class. Show and write the time math class starts.

Science Class   Math Class

_____ o'clock

Name _____

Practice

Learning Target: Use the hour hand to tell time to the hour.

An hour passes when the hour hand moves from one number to the next.

__3__ o'clock.

Write the time shown by the hour hand.

1.

_____ o'clock

2.

_____ o'clock

3.

_____ o'clock

Draw the hour hand to show the time.

4. 4 o'clock

5. 12 o'clock

6. 8 o'clock

Chapter 12 | Lesson 1   five hundred eighty-seven   587

7. **Precision** You eat a snack at 2 o'clock. Which clock shows the time you eat a snack?

8. **Modeling Real Life** Your friend gets on the bus 1 hour later than you. Show and write the time your friend gets on the bus.

You

Friend

_____ o'clock

9. **DIG DEEPER!** In Exercise 8, your cousin wakes up 2 hours before your friend gets on the bus. Write the time your cousin wakes up.

_____ o'clock

Review & Refresh

Use mental math.

10. $60 + 10 =$ _____

11. $23 + 10 =$ _____

Name _____

Learning Target: Use the hour hand to tell time to the half hour.

Tell Time to the Half Hour 12.2

Explore and Grow

Draw the hour hand and tell the time.

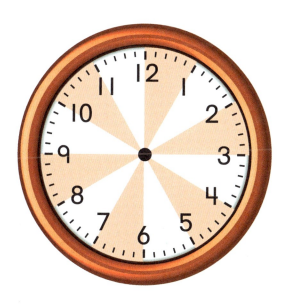

The hour hand points to the 3.

It is _____ o'clock.

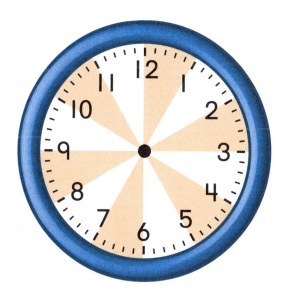

The hour hand points between the 3 and the 4.

It is half past _____.

Chapter 12 | Lesson 2

five hundred eighty-nine 589

Think and Grow

The hour hand is halfway between the 1 and the 2.

So, it is **half past** ____1____.

A **half hour** passes when the hour hand moves halfway to the next number.

Show and Grow — I can do it!

Write the time shown by the hour hand.

1.

   half past _____

2.

   half past _____

3.

   half past _____

4.

   half past _____

5.

   half past _____

6.

   half past _____

Name _____

✓ Apply and Grow: Practice

Write the time shown by the hour hand.

7.

half past _____

8.

half past _____

9.

_____ o'clock

Draw the hour hand to show the time.

10. half past 6

11. 1 o'clock

12. half past 9

13. **DIG DEEPER!** Is it time for lunch or recess?

Lunch: half past 11
Recess: half past 12

Repeated Reasoning
Where does the hour hand point when it is half past 11? half past 12?

Lunch   Recess

Chapter 12 | Lesson 2   five hundred ninety-one   **591**

Think and Grow: Modeling Real Life

Soccer practice lasts a half hour. Show and circle the time practice ends.

Start

End

half past 3   5 o'clock   half past 4

Show and Grow — I can think deeper!

14. A television show lasts a half hour. Show and circle the time the show ends.

Start

End

7 o'clock   half past 7   6 o'clock

Name _____

Practice 

Learning Target: Use the hour hand to tell time to the half hour.

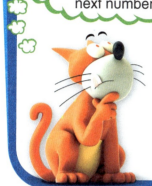

A half hour passes when the hour hand moves halfway to the next number.

half past __3__

Write the time shown by the hour hand.

1.

half past _____

2.

half past _____

3.

half past _____

Draw the hour hand to show the time.

4. half past 9

5. half past 2

6. 10 o'clock

Chapter 12 | Lesson 2

7. **DIG DEEPER!** Is it time for art class or math class?

Art class: half past 9
Math class: half past 10

Art class   Math class

8. **Modeling Real Life** Your music class lasts a half hour. Show and circle the time your music class ends.

Start   End

half past 12   half past 1   2 o'clock

Review & Refresh

9. Your friend has 9 peanuts. You have 2 fewer than your friend. How many peanuts do you have?

Friend: ☐

You: ☐

_____ ◯ _____ = _____

_____ peanuts

594   five hundred ninety-four

Name _____

Tell Time to the Hour and Half Hour

Learning Target: Use the hour and minute hands to tell time to the hour and half hour.

Complete the sentences.

The hour hand points to the _____.

The minute hand points to the _____.

It is _____ o'clock.

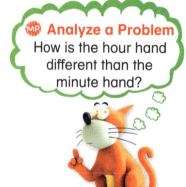

Analyze a Problem
How is the hour hand different than the minute hand?

The hour hand points halfway between

the _____ and the _____.

The minute hand points to the _____.

It is half past _____.

Chapter 12 | **Lesson 3**

five hundred ninety-five 595

Think and Grow

4 o'clock   half past 4

The **minute hand** is longer than the hour hand. It shows the **minute**.

Show and Grow — I can do it!

Write the time.

1.

2.

3.

4.

5.

6.

596   five hundred ninety-six

Name _____

 Apply and Grow: Practice

Draw to show the time.

7. half past 5

8. 6 o'clock

9. half past 10

10. 3 o'clock

11. 11 o'clock

12. half past 4

13. **YOU BE THE TEACHER** Newton shows half past 6. Is he correct? Explain.

_____
_____
_____
_____

Chapter 12 | Lesson 3 five hundred ninety-seven **597**

Think and Grow: Modeling Real Life

You spend an hour at the park.
Show and write the time you leave.

Arrive   Leave

  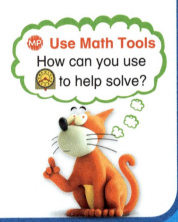

Use Math Tools
How can you use 🕐 to help solve?

_____

Show and Grow   I can think deeper!

14. You spend a half hour on your homework.
Show and write the time you finish.

Start   Finish

_____

Name _____

Practice 12.3

Learning Target: Use the hour and minute hands to tell time to the hour and half hour.

8 o'clock

half past 8

Write the time.

1.
   _____

2.
   _____

3.
   _____

Draw to show the time.

4. 5 o'clock

5. half past 7

6. half past 2

Chapter 12 | Lesson 3

7. **YOU BE THE TEACHER** Descartes shows 12 o'clock. Is he correct? Explain.

_____
_____
_____

8. **Modeling Real Life** You play tag for an hour. Show and write the time you stop playing tag.

Start   Stop

_____

9. **DIG DEEPER!** You play hide-and-seek for one and a half hours. Show and write the time you stop playing hide-and-seek.

Start   Stop

_____

Review & Refresh

Count by ones to write the missing numbers.

10. 43, ____, ____, ____, ____, ____

Name _____

Learning Target: Use analog and digital clocks to tell time.

Tell Time Using Analog and Digital Clocks

12.4

Explore and Grow

Show the time on the analog clock. What is the same about the clocks? What is different?

The time is _____ o'clock.

The time is half past _____.

Chapter 12 | Lesson 4

six hundred one 601

Think and Grow

A half hour is 30 minutes.

↑
digital clock

An hour is 60 minutes.

Show and Grow   I can do it!

Show the time.

1.

2.

3.

4.

Name _____

 Apply and Grow: Practice

Show the time.

5.

6.

Draw to show the time.

7.

8.

DIG DEEPER! Complete the clocks to show the same time.

9.

10.

11. **Which One Doesn't Belong?** Which time does not belong with the other three? Think: How do you know?

   half past 3

Chapter 12 | Lesson 4   six hundred three   603

Think and Grow: Modeling Real Life

A play starts 1 hour later than a movie. Show and circle the time the play starts.

Movie

Play

half past 2   half past 4   3 o'clock   4 o'clock

Show and Grow — I can think deeper!

12. Tumbling starts a half hour later than dance. Show and circle the time tumbling starts.

Dance

Tumbling

half past 5   4 o'clock   6 o'clock   half past 4

Name _____

Practice

Learning Target: Use analog and digital clocks to tell time.

Show the time.

1.

2.

3.

Draw to show the time.

4.

5.

6.

Chapter 12 | Lesson 4   six hundred five   605

7. **Which One Doesn't Belong?** Which time does not belong with the other three? Think: How do you know?

   half past 6

8. **Modeling Real Life** Bowling starts 1 hour later than ice skating. Show and circle the time bowling starts.

Ice Skating

Bowling

half past 5   5 o'clock   half past 4   3 o'clock

9. **Reasoning** As the minute hand moves from the 12 to the 6, how much time passes?

Review & Refresh

10. Circle the cone. Draw a rectangle around the cylinder.

Performance Task 12

1. Your class is on a field trip to a nature center. Complete the schedule.

   a. The Pond Study starts at the time shown.

   b. The Wildlife Walk starts at half past 9.

   c. The Scavenger Hunt starts 1 hour after the Wildlife Walk starts.

   d. Recess starts a half hour after lunch.

   e. You leave 1 hour before 3:00.

   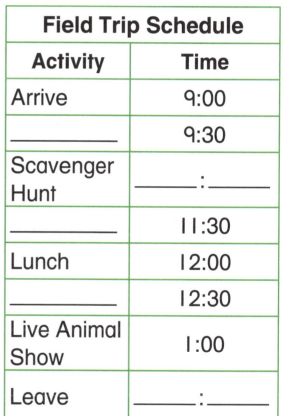

Field Trip Schedule	
Activity	Time
Arrive	9:00
_____	9:30
Scavenger Hunt	____:____
_____	11:30
Lunch	12:00
_____	12:30
Live Animal Show	1:00
Leave	____:____

2. Lunch lasts a half hour. Write the time that lunch ends.

3. Draw the time the Live Animal Show starts.

Time Flip and Find

To Play: Place the Time Flip and Find Cards facedown in the boxes. Take turns flipping 2 cards. If your cards show the same time, keep the cards. If your cards show different times, flip the cards back over. Play until all matches are made.

Name _____

Chapter Practice 12

12.1 Tell Time to the Hour

Write the time shown by the hour hand.

1.

   _____ o'clock

2.

   _____ o'clock

3.

   _____ o'clock

12.2 Tell Time to the Half Hour

Draw the hour hand to show the time.

4. half past 9

5. 2 o'clock

6. half past 5

7. **Precision** Is it time to brush your teeth or go to bed?

   Brush teeth: half past 7
   Go to bed: half past 8

   Brush teeth

   Go to bed

Chapter 12 — six hundred nine — 609

12.3 Tell Time to the Hour and Half Hour

Write the time.

8.
_____

9.
_____

10.
_____

11. **Modeling Real Life** You read for a half hour. Show and write the time you stop reading.

Start

Stop

_____

12.4 Tell Time Using Analog and Digital Clocks

Complete the clocks to show the same time.

12.

13.

14.

13 Two- and Three-Dimensional Shapes

- Have you ever built a sandcastle?
- What shapes do you see?

Chapter Learning Target:
Understand two- and three-dimensional shapes.

Chapter Success Criteria:
- I can identify shapes.
- I can describe two- and three-dimensional shapes.
- I can compare shapes.
- I can create shapes.

13 Vocabulary

Name _____

Review Words
hexagon
square

Organize It

Use the review words to complete the graphic organizer.

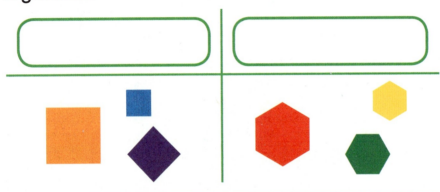

Define It

Use your vocabulary cards to identify the words. Find each word in the word search.

1.

2.

3.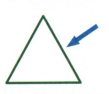

```
T  F  S  P  E  Z  U  I  D
Y  H  I  P  D  I  R  E  L
V  O  D  U  Z  S  V  P  D
E  M  E  H  O  L  B  A  S
R  R  I  L  M  C  K  U  T
T  U  K  S  F  T  O  T  K
E  S  U  L  Z  F  A  C  B
X  I  S  F  N  C  E  R  U
D  M  E  D  G  E  T  S  N
```

612 six hundred twelve

Chapter 13 Vocabulary Cards

curved surface	edge
flat surface	rectangular prism
rhombus	side
three-dimensional shape	trapezoid

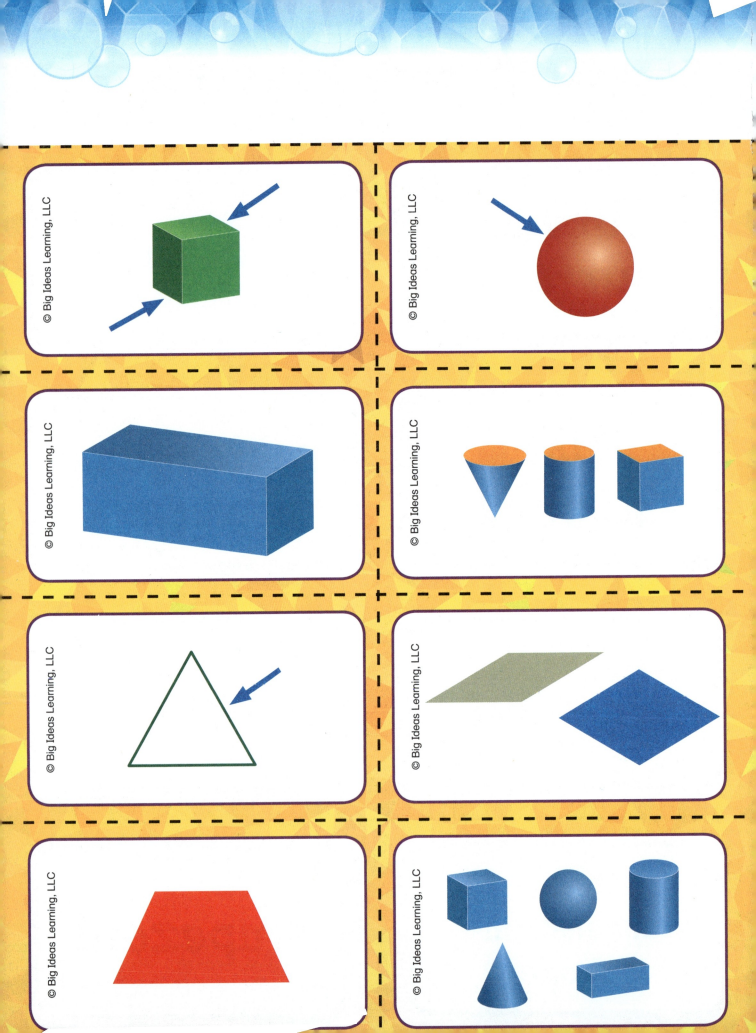

Chapter 13 Vocabulary Cards

two-dimensional shape

vertex

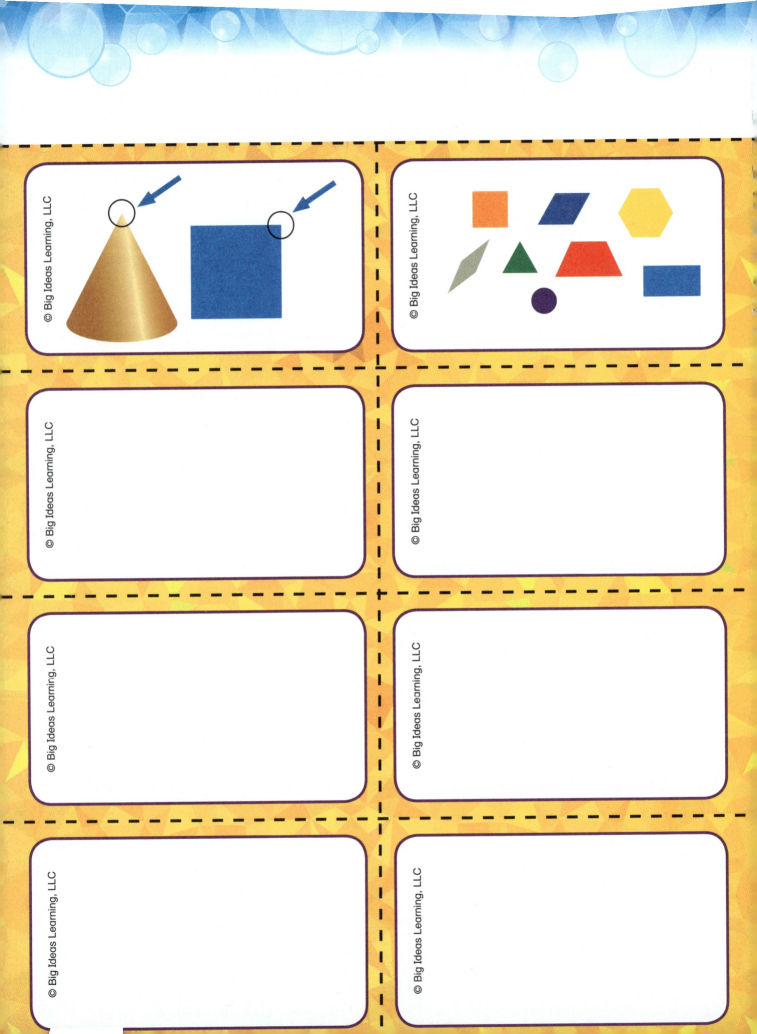

Sort Two-Dimensional Shapes

13.1

Learning Target: Sort two-dimensional shapes.

Sort the Shape Sort Cards. Explain how you sorted.

Compare Arguments
How did your partner sort? Did they sort correctly?

Chapter 13 | Lesson 1

Think and Grow

You can sort **two-dimensional shapes** in many ways.

Closed or Open
Closed

Open
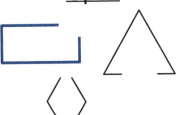

Number of Sides
3 sides

side →

Number of Vertices
4 vertices

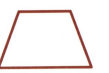
vertex →

Show and Grow — I can do it!

1. Circle the closed shapes with 4 vertices.

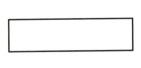 
 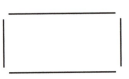

2. Circle the closed shapes with no straight sides.

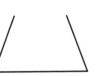

Name _____

3. Circle the closed shapes with only 3 vertices.

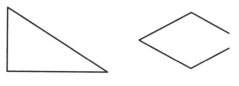

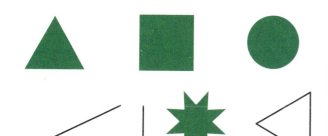

4. Circle the closed shapes with only L-shaped vertices.

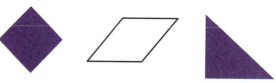

5. Circle the shapes with more than 4 straight sides.

6. Circle the shapes with 6 straight sides.

7. **DIG DEEPER!** Draw 2 different two-dimensional shapes that have only 4 straight sides.

Chapter 13 | Lesson 1   six hundred fifteen   **615**

Think and Grow: Modeling Real Life

Use the clues to color the picture.

Only 3 straight sides: **blue**　　Only 4 straight sides: **green**
No straight sides: **yellow**　　More than 4 vertices: **red**

Show and Grow　　I can think deeper!

8. Use the clues to color the picture.

   Only 3 vertices: **green**

   All L-shaped vertices: **orange**

   Only 4 straight sides and
   　no L-shaped vertices: **blue**

   6 straight sides: **yellow**

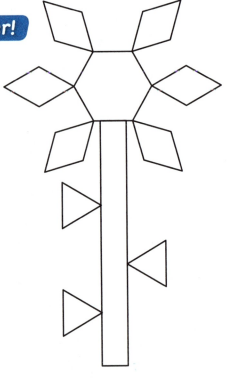

Name _____

Practice 13.1

Learning Target: Sort two-dimensional shapes.

You can sort two-dimensional shapes in many ways.

Closed or Open

Closed   Open

Number of Sides

<u>4</u> sides

Number of Vertices

<u>3</u> vertices

1. Circle the closed shapes with no straight sides.

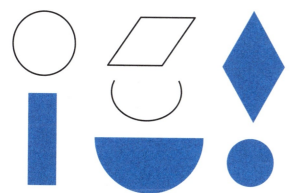

2. Circle the closed shapes with 4 sides of the same length.

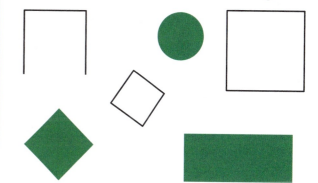

3. Circle the shapes with no vertices.

  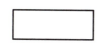

4. Circle the shapes with more than 4 vertices.

Chapter 13 | Lesson 1

six hundred seventeen 617

5. **DIG DEEPER!** Draw 2 different two-dimensional shapes with 2 long straight sides and 2 short straight sides.

6. **Modeling Real Life** Use the clues to color the picture.

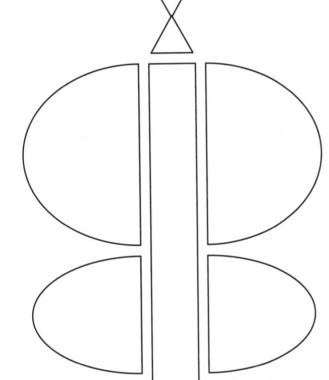

Only 3 vertices: **yellow**

Only 4 sides: **black**

Only 1 straight side: **orange**

No straight sides: **blue**

Check Your Work
How can you work backward to check your work?

Review & Refresh

7. Circle the longer object.

Name _____

Learning Target: Describe two-dimensional shapes.

Describe Two-Dimensional Shapes 13.2

Explore and Grow

Which shape has three sides?

Which shapes have 4 sides and 4 L-shaped vertices?

Which shapes have 4 sides and no L-shaped vertices?

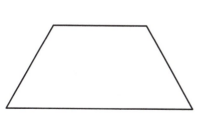 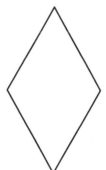 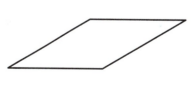

Use your materials to build each shape you circled.

Chapter 13 | Lesson 2   six hundred nineteen   619

Think and Grow

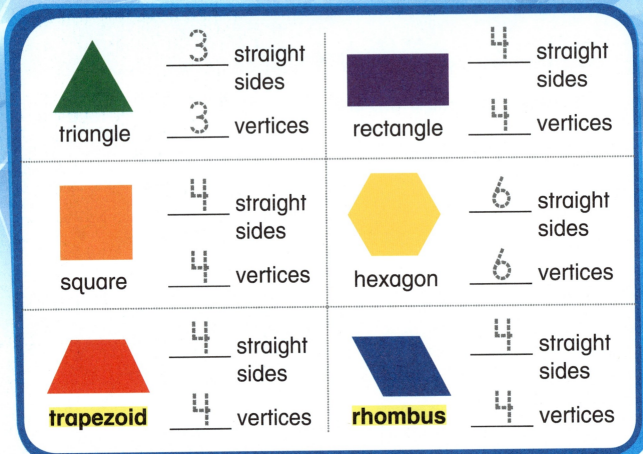

Show and Grow I can do it!

1.  _____ straight sides
_____ vertices

2. 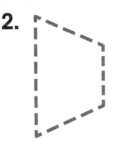 _____ straight sides
_____ vertices

3.  _____ straight sides
_____ vertices

4. _____ straight sides
_____ vertices

Apply and Grow: Practice

5. 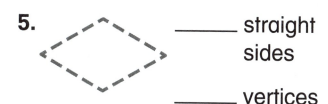 _____ straight sides

_____ vertices

6. 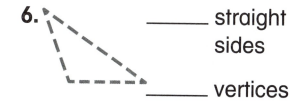 _____ straight sides

_____ vertices

7.  _____ straight sides

_____ vertices

8. 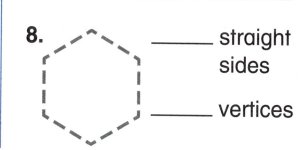 _____ straight sides

_____ vertices

Circle the attributes of the shape.

9. **Triangle**

0 straight sides

3 straight sides

3 vertices

open

10. **Square**

6 straight sides of the same length

4 straight sides of the same length

4 vertices

closed

11. **Precision** Match each shape with an attribute that describes it.

| Circle | Rectangle | Hexagon |

| 6 straight sides | 0 vertices | only 4 vertices |

Chapter 13 | Lesson 2   six hundred twenty-one   621

Think and Grow: Modeling Real Life

A board game has 4 sides and 4 L-shaped vertices. Name and draw two shapes for the board game.

Circle: Square   Hexagon   Trapezoid   Rectangle

Draw shapes:

Show and Grow — I can think deeper!

12. A board game has 4 sides and no L-shaped vertices. Name and draw two shapes for the board game.

    Circle: Triangle   Trapezoid   Rhombus   Square

    Draw shapes:

Modeling Real Life
Describe the shape of your favorite board game to a partner.

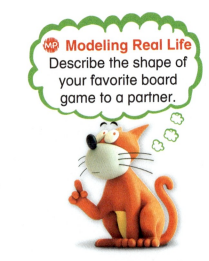

Name _____

Practice 13.2

Learning Target: Describe two-dimensional shapes.

 __4__ straight sides
__4__ vertices

 __3__ straight sides
__3__ vertices

1.  ____ straight sides
____ vertices

2.  ____ straight sides
____ vertices

3.  ____ straight sides
____ vertices

4.  ____ straight sides
____ vertices

Circle the attributes of the shape.

5. **Trapezoid**

    4 straight sides

    6 straight sides

    5 vertices

    closed

6. **Rectangle**

    4 straight sides

    0 vertices

    4 vertices

    open

Chapter 13 | Lesson 2

7. **Precision** Match each shape with an attribute that describes it.

   Triangle   Trapezoid   Circle

   only 3 straight sides   0 straight sides   4 vertices

8. **Modeling Real Life** A photograph has 4 straight sides of the same length and 4 vertices. Draw and name two possible shapes for the photograph.

   _____   _____

9. **DIG DEEPER!** Draw three triangles that are not touching. How many vertices are there in all? Write an equation to match.

Review & Refresh

10. Complete the tally chart.

Milk Choice	
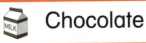 Chocolate	
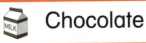 Strawberry	
White	

Combine Two-Dimensional Shapes

13.3

Learning Target: Join two-dimensional shapes to make another shape.

Use 2 triangles to make a new two-dimensional shape. Draw your shape.

Use 3 triangles to make a new two-dimensional shape. Draw your shape.

Chapter 13 | Lesson 3

six hundred twenty-five 625

Think and Grow

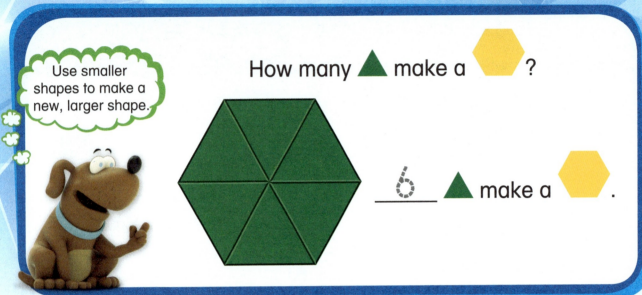

Use smaller shapes to make a new, larger shape.

How many ▲ make a ⬢ ?

__6__ ▲ make a ⬢.

Show and Grow — I can do it!

1. How many 🟥 make a 🟨 ?

   _____ 🟥 make a 🟨.

2. How many 🔷 make a 🟨 ?

   _____ 🔷 make a 🟨.

3. How many 🟣 make a 🔴 ?

   _____ 🟣 make a 🔴.

4. How many 🔸 make a 🟧 ?

   _____ 🔸 make a 🟧.

Name _____

✓ Apply and Grow: Practice

5. How many 🔺 make a 🟥?

_____ 🔺 make a 🟥.

6. How many 🟧 make a ▬?

_____ 🟧 make a ▬.

7. Draw the shape you can use 2 times to make a ⬡.

8. Draw the shape you can use 3 times to make a ⬡.

9. Choose Tools Which shape can you use 2 times to make a ▱?

10. DIG DEEPER! Draw to show 2 different ways you can use pattern blocks to make the shape.

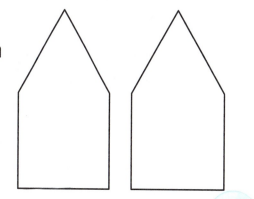

Chapter 13 | Lesson 3   six hundred twenty-seven   **627**

Think and Grow: Modeling Real Life

Use the number of pattern blocks to fill the shape on the sign. How many of each block do you use? Draw to show your work.

3 blocks:

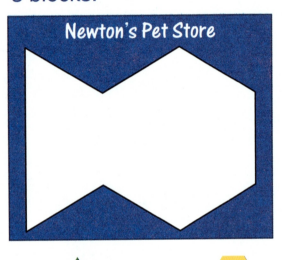

4 blocks:

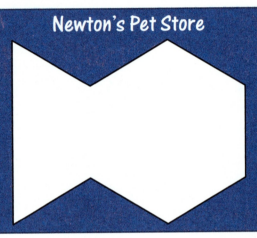

Show and Grow   I can think deeper!

11. Use 3 pattern blocks to fill the shape on the sign. How many of each block do you use? Draw to show your work.

Name _____

Practice 13.3

Learning Target: Join two-dimensional shapes to make another shape.

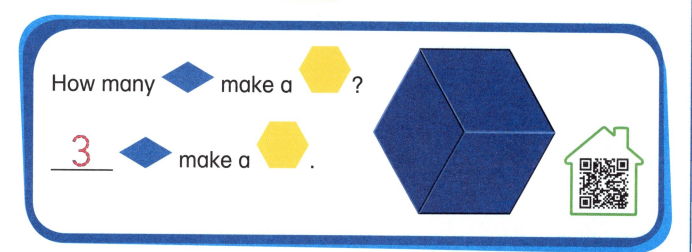

How many 🔷 make a ⬡ ?

__3__ 🔷 make a ⬡.

1. How many 🔺 make a 🔷?

    🔺 make a 🔷.

2. How many ╱ make a ＜ ?

   _____ ╱ make a ＜.

3. How many 🔺 make a ⬡ ?

    🔺 make a ⬡.

4. How many ⌒ make a ⌒ ?

    ⌒ make a ⌒.

Chapter 13 | Lesson 3   six hundred twenty-nine   629

5. **Choose Tools** Which 2 pattern blocks can you use to make the shape?

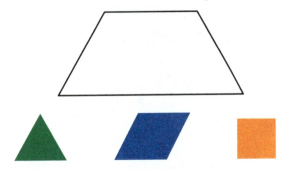

6. **DIG DEEPER!** Draw to show 2 different ways you can use pattern blocks to make a larger △.

7. **Modeling Real Life** Use 5 pattern blocks to fill the shape on the sign. How many of each block do you use? Draw to show your work.

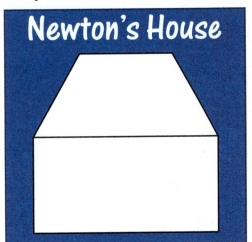

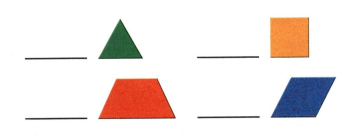

Review & Refresh

Write the time.

8.

____ : ____ ____

9.

____ : ____ ____

Name _____

Create More Shapes 13.4

Learning Target: Join two-dimensional shapes to make a new shape. Use the new shape to make a larger shape.

Use two or more shapes to make the center of the flower. Use more shapes to fill in the rest of the flower.

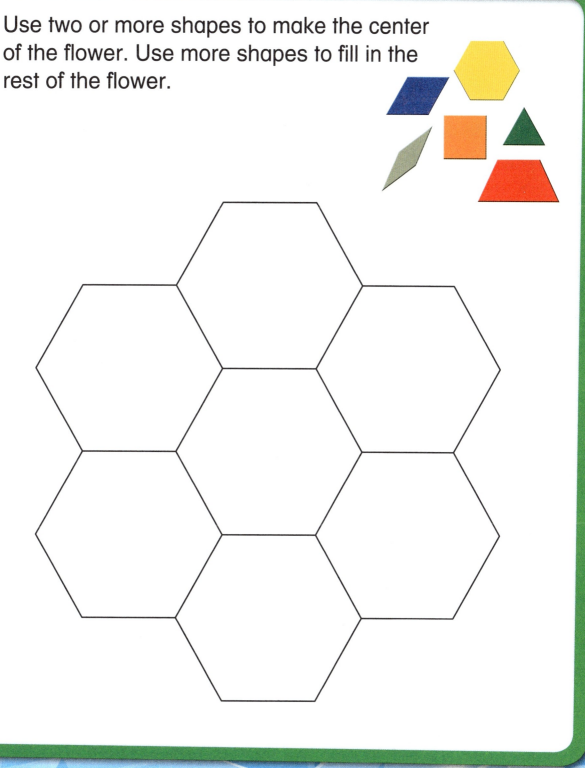

Chapter 13 | Lesson 4   six hundred thirty-one   631

Think and Grow

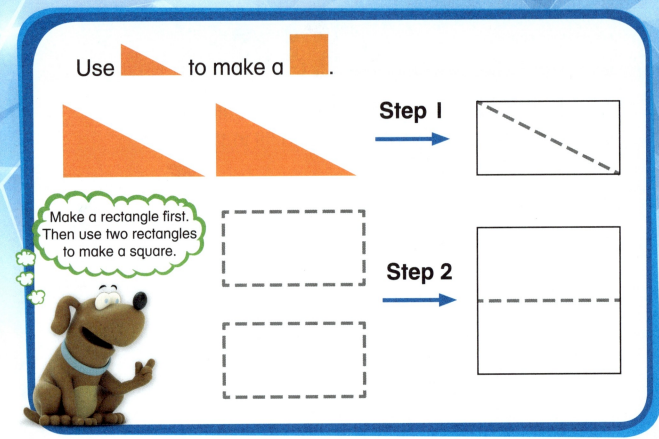

Show and Grow — I can do it!

1. Use 🟦 to make a 🔴. Draw to show your work.

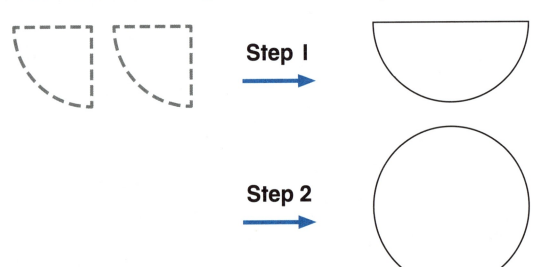

Apply and Grow: Practice

2. Use △ to make a ▭. Draw to show your work.

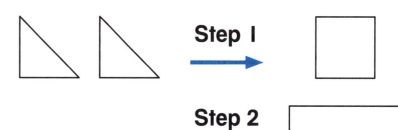

3. Use △ and ⬠ to make a ▱. Draw to show your work.

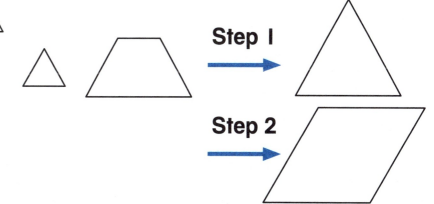

4. Draw the shape you can use 3 times to make a ⌓.

5. Draw the shape you can use 4 times to make a △.

6. **DIG DEEPER!** Draw to show two different ways you can join the shapes on the left to make the larger shape.

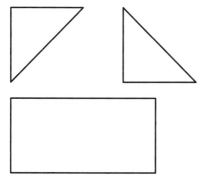
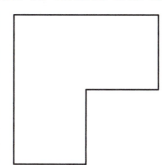
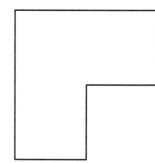

Chapter 13 | Lesson 4
six hundred thirty-three 633

Think and Grow: Modeling Real Life

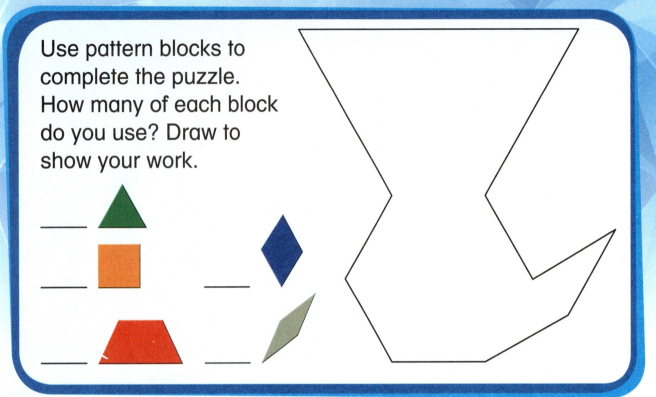

Use pattern blocks to complete the puzzle. How many of each block do you use? Draw to show your work.

Show and Grow — I can think deeper!

7. Use pattern blocks to complete the puzzle. How many of each block do you use? Draw to show your work.

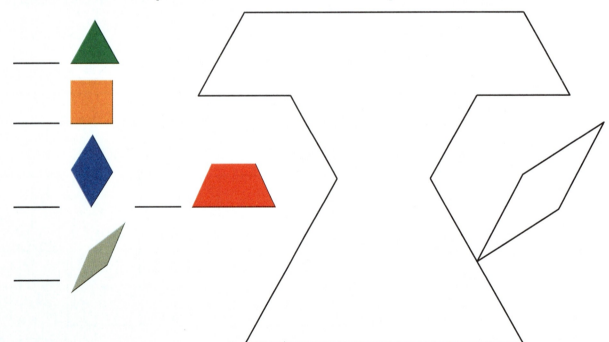

634   six hundred thirty-four

Name _____

Practice 13.4

Learning Target: Join two-dimensional shapes to make a new shape. Use the new shape to make a larger shape.

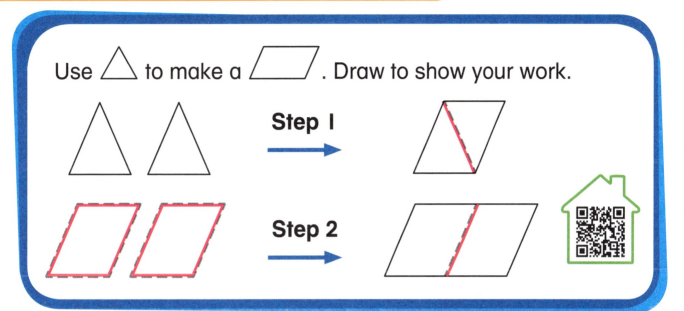

1. Use ▢ to make a larger ▢. Draw to show your work.

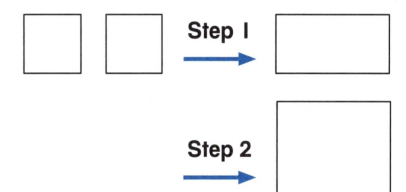

2. Use ◣ to make a ◆. Draw to show your work.

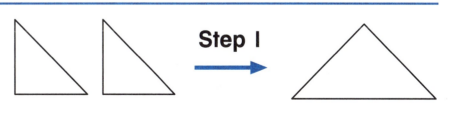

Chapter 13 | Lesson 4   six hundred thirty-five   635

3. **DIG DEEPER!** Draw to show two ways you can combine the 3 shapes on the left to make the larger shape.

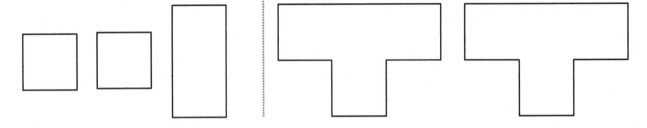

4. **Modeling Real Life** Use pattern blocks to complete the puzzle. How many of each block do you use? Draw to show your work.

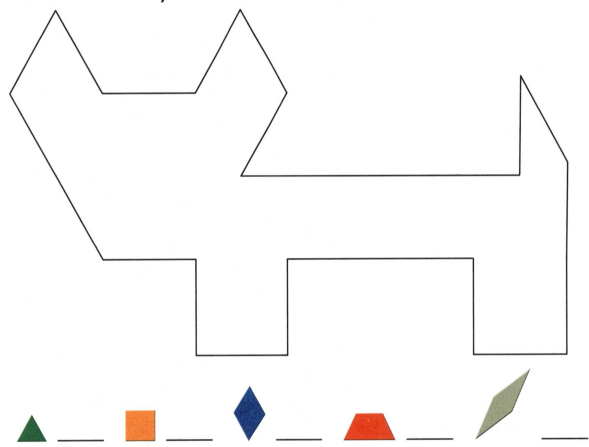

Review & Refresh

5. ___ is greater than 17
   ___ is less than 19.

6. ___ is greater than 12
   ___ is less than 11.

Name _____

Learning Target: Take apart two-dimensional shapes.

Take Apart Two-Dimensional Shapes 13.5

Explore and Grow

Draw lines to take apart each figure.

Show two rectangles.

Show four squares.

Show 2 triangles and 1 rectangle.

Show 2 triangles and 2 squares.

Chapter 13 | Lesson 5

six hundred thirty-seven 637

Think and Grow

Draw one line to show 2 rectangles.

Here are two more ways.

Show and Grow I can do it!

Draw one line to show the parts.

1. 2 triangles

2. 2 triangles

3. 2 trapezoids

4. 1 triangle and 1 trapezoid

Name _____

 Apply and Grow: Practice

Draw one line to show the parts.

5. 2 triangles

6. 2 squares

Draw two lines to show the parts.

7. 2 triangles and 1 trapezoid

8. 2 triangles and 1 rectangle

9. **Reasoning** Show how to use the shapes to make the hexagon.

1

3

2

2

10. **Reasoning** Show how to use the shapes to make a circle. How many of each shape do you use?

Chapter 13 | Lesson 5

Think and Grow: Modeling Real Life

How many squares can you find on the Four Square court?

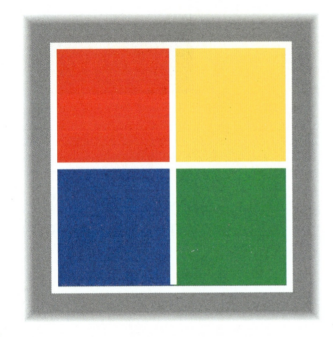

_____ squares

Show and Grow   I can think deeper!

11. How many squares can you find on the magic square?

2	7	6
9	5	1
4	3	8

_____ squares

Name _____

Practice  13.5

Learning Target: Take apart two-dimensional shapes.

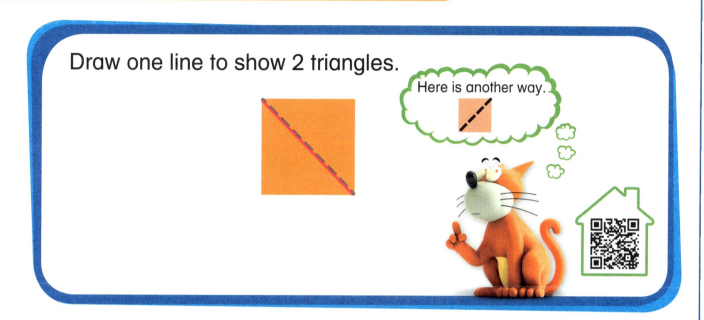

Draw one line to show 2 triangles.

Draw one line to show the parts.

1. 2 trapezoids

2. 1 rectangle and 1 square

Draw two lines to show the parts.

3. 3 triangles

4. 1 rectangle and 2 triangles

Chapter 13 | Lesson 5   six hundred forty-one 641

5. **Reasoning** Show how to use the shapes to make the ▱.

6. **DIG DEEPER!** You take apart a shape. You are left with a trapezoid and 3 triangles with equal side lengths. Write the name of the shape you started with.

7. **Modeling Real Life** How many triangles are in Descartes's design?

_____ triangles

Review & Refresh

8. Circle the three-dimensional shapes. Draw rectangles around the two-dimensional shapes.

Name _____

Learning Target: Sort three-dimensional shapes.

Sort Three-Dimensional Shapes
13.6

Sort the Three-Dimensional Shape Cards. Explain how you sorted.

Chapter 13 | Lesson 6

six hundred forty-three 643

Think and Grow

You can sort **three-dimensional shapes** in many ways.

Only Flat Surfaces — flat surface

Only a Curved Surface — curved surface

Show and Grow I can do it!

1. Circle the shapes with flat surfaces that are circles.

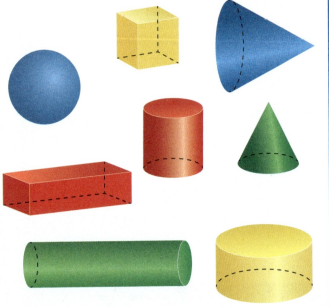

2. Circle the shapes with both flat and curved surfaces.

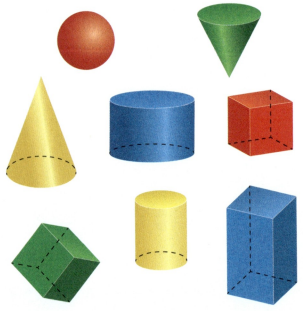

644 six hundred forty-four

Name _____

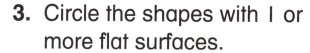

3. Circle the shapes with 1 or more flat surfaces.

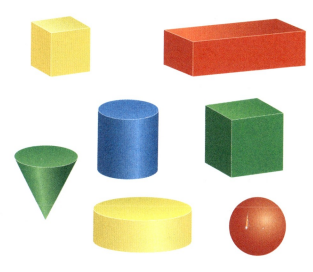

4. Circle the shapes with a curved surface.

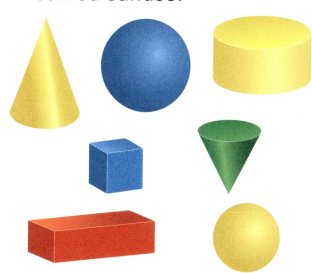

5. Circle the shapes with only 2 flat surfaces.

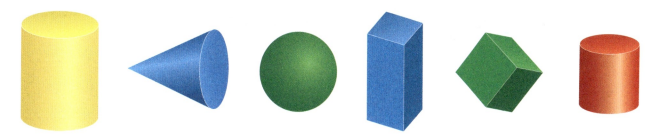

6. **Structure** Match each shape to its group.

only flat surfaces   both flat and curved surfaces   only a curved surface

Chapter 13 | Lesson 6   six hundred forty-five   645

Think and Grow: Modeling Real Life

You need to find an object that has no flat surfaces for a scavenger hunt. Circle the objects you can use.

Show and Grow   I can think deeper!

7. You need to find an object that has only two flat surfaces for a scavenger hunt. Circle the objects you can use.

Name _____

Practice 13.6

Learning Target: Sort three-dimensional shapes.

You can sort three-dimensional shapes in many ways.

Flat Surfaces that are Rectangles	Flat Surfaces that are Circles

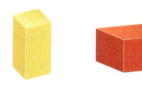 

1. Circle the shapes with no flat surface.

2. Circle the shapes with flat surfaces that are rectangles.

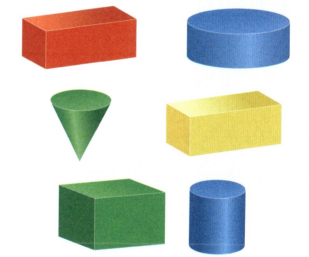

3. Circle the shapes with more than 2 flat surfaces.

Chapter 13 | Lesson 6   six hundred forty-seven   647

4. **Structure** Match each shape to its group.

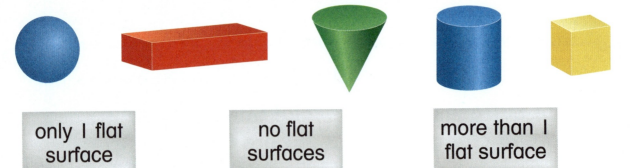

only 1 flat surface · no flat surfaces · more than 1 flat surface

5. **Modeling Real Life** You need to find an object that has both flat and curved surfaces for a scavenger hunt. Circle the objects you can use.

6. **DIG DEEPER!** Compare the shapes. How are they the same? How are they different?

_____

_____

Review & Refresh

7. $30 + 30 = $ _____

8. $60 + 20 = $ _____

Name _____

Learning Target: Describe three-dimensional shapes.

Describe Three-Dimensional Shapes

13.7

Explore and Grow

Use your materials to build one of the three-dimensional shapes shown. Circle the shape you make. How many flat surfaces does your shape have? How many vertices does your shape have?

_____ flat surfaces

_____ vertices

Chapter 13 | Lesson 7

six hundred forty-nine 649

Think and Grow

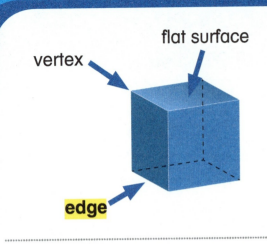

cube

___6___ flat surfaces
___8___ vertices
___12___ edges

rectangular prism

___6___ flat surfaces
___8___ vertices
___12___ edges

cylinder

___2___ flat surfaces
___0___ vertices
___0___ edges

cone

___1___ flat surface
___1___ vertices
___0___ edges

sphere

___0___ flat surfaces
___0___ vertices
___0___ edges

Show and Grow — I can do it!

1.  ____ flat surfaces   ____ vertices   ____ edges

six hundred fifty

Name _____

✓ Apply and Grow: Practice

2.  _____ flat surfaces

   _____ vertices

   _____ edges

3.  _____ flat surfaces

   _____ vertices

   _____ edges

Circle the attributes of the shape.

4. **Cone**

   1 flat surface

   0 vertices

   slides

   two-dimensional

5. **Cube**

   6 flat surfaces

   12 vertices

   12 edges

   rolls

6. I am a three-dimensional shape that has no flat surfaces, no vertices, and no edges. What am I?

   _____

7. I am a three-dimensional shape that has 1 flat surface, 1 vertex, and no edges. What am I?

   _____

8. **DIG DEEPER!** Newton buys an item that has 2 more flat surfaces than edges. Which item does he buy?

Chapter 13 | Lesson 7   six hundred fifty-one 651

Think and Grow: Modeling Real Life

Circle the object below the table that has 0 flat surfaces. Draw a line through the object above the basketball that has 12 edges.

Show and Grow   I can think deeper!

9. Circle the object in front of the campers that has more than 2 flat surfaces. Draw a line through the object behind the logs that has 1 vertex and 1 flat surface.

Name _____

Practice 13.7

Learning Target: Describe three-dimensional shapes.

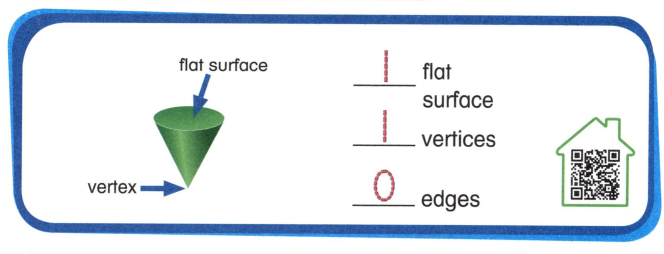

1. _____ flat surfaces
   _____ vertices
   _____ edges

2. _____ flat surfaces
   _____ vertices
   _____ edges

3. Circle the shape that has the same number of vertices as edges.

4. Circle the shape that has the same number of flat surfaces as vertices.

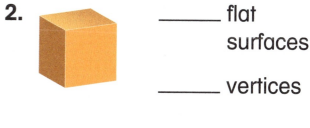

Circle the attributes of the shape.

5. **Cylinder**

   2 flat surfaces

   3 flat surfaces

   2 vertices

   stacks

6. **Rectangular Prism**

   8 flat surfaces

   12 edges

   slides

   three-dimensional

Chapter 13 | Lesson 7

7. **DIG DEEPER!** Descartes buys an item that has 2 fewer flat surfaces than vertices. Which item does he buy?

8. **MP Repeated Reasoning** What other shape has the same number of surfaces, vertices, and edges as a rectangular prism? How is that shape different from a rectangular prism?

_____

_____

9. **MP Modeling Real Life** Circle the object next to the hat that has 6 square flat surfaces. Draw a line through the object in front of the hat that has 0 edges and 1 vertex.

Review & Refresh

10. 20 + 18 = _____

11. 40 + 25 = _____

Name _____

Combine Three-Dimensional Shapes 13.8

Learning Target: Join three-dimensional shapes to make another shape.

 Explore and Grow

Which three-dimensional shapes can you make using cubes? Build one of the shapes.

Chapter 13 | Lesson 8

six hundred fifty-five 655

Think and Grow

Use the rectangular prisms to make a new shape.

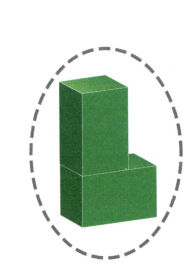

Show and Grow I can do it!

Circle the new shape that you can make.

1.

2.

Apply and Grow: Practice

Circle the new shape that you can make.

3.

4.

5.

6. **DIG DEEPER!** How many cubes do you need in all to make the next shape?

      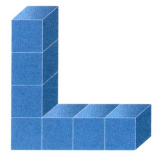   ?

_____ cubes

Chapter 13 | Lesson 8 six hundred fifty-seven **657**

Think and Grow: Modeling Real Life

You build a wall. It is 5 cubes long and 2 cubes tall. Your friend builds a wall. It is 4 cubes long and 2 cubes tall. How many more cubes do you use than your friend?

Draw pictures: You   Friend

Equation:

_____ more cubes

Show and Grow I can think deeper!

7. You build a wall. It is 3 cubes long and 3 cubes tall. Your friend builds a wall. It is 5 cubes long and 3 cubes tall. How many more cubes does your friend use than you?

Draw pictures: You   Friend

Equation:

_____ more cubes

Name _____

Practice 13.8

Learning Target: Join three-dimensional shapes to make another shape.

Circle the new shape that you can make.

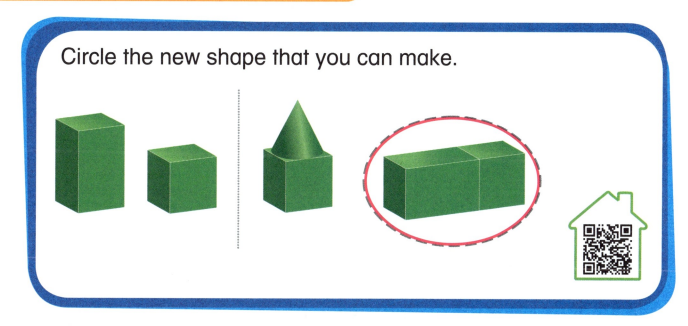

Circle the new shape that you can make.

1.

2.

Chapter 13 | Lesson 8 six hundred fifty-nine 659

3. **DIG DEEPER!** How many cubes do you need in all to make the next shape?

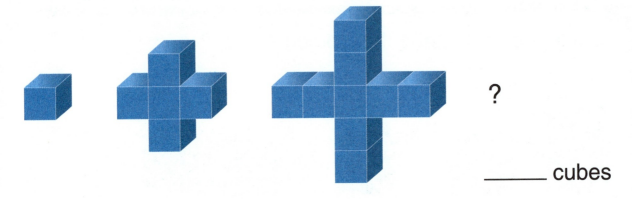

_____ cubes

4. **Modeling Real Life** You build a wall that is 2 cubes long and 4 cubes tall. Your friend builds a wall that is 4 cubes long and 3 cubes tall. How many more cubes does your friend use than you?

_____ more cubes

Review & Refresh

5. Order from shortest to longest.

green

yellow

black

_____, _____, _____

Name _____

Learning Target: Take apart three-dimensional shapes.

Take Apart Three-Dimensional Shapes

13.9

Explore and Grow

Circle the three-dimensional shapes used to build the castle.

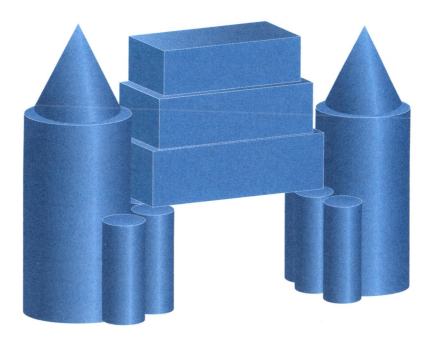

Chapter 13 | Lesson 9

six hundred sixty-one 661

Think and Grow

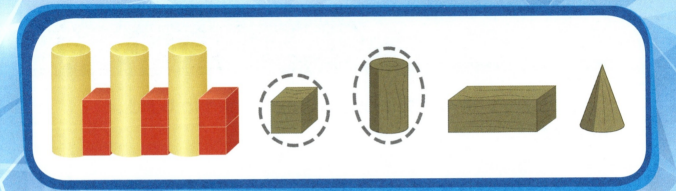

Show and Grow   I can do it!

Circle the shapes that make up the structure.

1.

2.

3.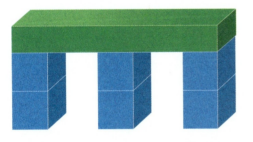

4.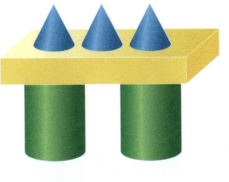

Name _____

✓ Apply and Grow: Practice

Circle the shapes that make up the structure.

5.

6.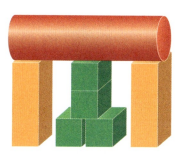

7.

8.

9. **MP Reasoning** Which two structures are the same?

Chapter 13 | Lesson 9   six hundred sixty-three   663

Think and Grow: Modeling Real Life

How many of each shape make up the gate?

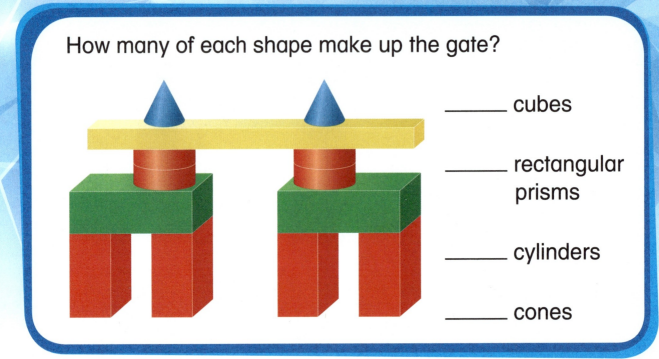

_____ cubes

_____ rectangular prisms

_____ cylinders

_____ cones

Show and Grow   I can think deeper!

10. How many of each shape make up the bridge?

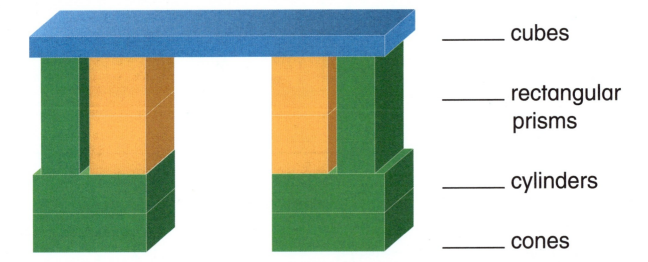

_____ cubes

_____ rectangular prisms

_____ cylinders

_____ cones

Name _____

Practice  **13.9**

Learning Target: Take apart three-dimensional shapes.

Circle the shapes that make up the structure.

Circle the shapes that make up the structure.

1.

2.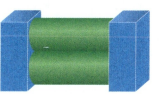

3.

4.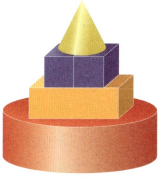

5. **Reasoning** Which two structures are the same?

6. **Modeling Real Life** How many of each shape make up the castle?

_____ cubes

_____ rectangular prisms

_____ cylinders

_____ cones

7. **DIG DEEPER!** Circle the names of the shapes that do *not* make up the desk.

sphere   rectangular prism

cylinder   cone

Review & Refresh

8. 12 + 7 = _____   **9.** 42 + 14 = _____

Name _____

Performance Task 13

1. Use the clues to finish the two-dimensional sand castle drawing.

   - The flag on the castle is a closed shape with only 3 straight sides.
   - The handle of the shovel is a closed shape with L-shaped vertices and 4 sides of the same length.
   - The window on the castle is a closed shape with only 6 straight sides.
   - The door on the castle is a closed shape with 4 sides that you can use 2 times to make a square.

2. You are building a sand castle using these three-dimensional shapes.

   - 4 shapes that have square flat surfaces
   - 5 shapes that have 2 flat surfaces and no vertices
   - 3 shapes that have the same number of flat surfaces as vertices

   a. Which shape is missing from the sand castle?

   b. Color a flat surface to show where you would stack the missing shape to complete the sand castle.

Chapter 13   six hundred sixty-seven   667

Shape Roll and Build

To Play: Roll a die to choose a pattern block. Cover a shape in the picture. Keep rolling until all shapes have been covered.

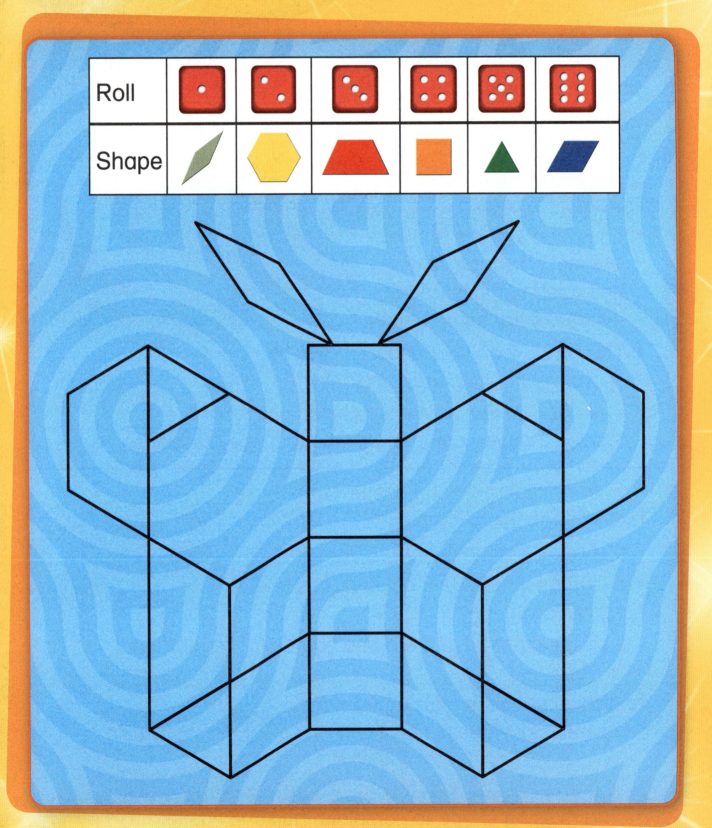

Name _____

Chapter Practice 13

13.1 Sort Two-Dimensional Shapes

1. Circle the closed shapes with only 3 straight sides.

2. **MP Structure** Draw 2 different two-dimensional shapes that have 1 or more L-shaped vertices.

13.2 Describe Two-Dimensional Shapes

Circle the attributes of the shape.

3. **Hexagon**

   6 straight sides

   8 straight sides

   8 vertices

   closed

4. **Rhombus**

   4 straight sides

   4 vertices

   6 vertices

   open

Chapter 13 · six hundred sixty-nine 669

13.3 Combine Two-Dimensional Shapes

5. How many make a ?

_____ ▲ make a ⬢.

6. How many ▲ make a

_____ ▲ make a .

13.4 Create More Shapes

7. Use △ to make a ▯. Draw to show your work.

 Step 1 ➡ Step 2 ➡

8. Use ◜ and □ to make a ⌂. Draw to show your work.

  Step 1 ➡ Step 2 ➡

670   six hundred seventy

13.5 Take Apart Two-Dimensional Shapes

Draw two lines to show the parts.

9. 1 square and 2 triangles

10. 2 triangles and 1 square

 13.6 Sort Three-Dimensional Shapes

11. Circle the shapes with flat surfaces that are all squares.

12. **Modeling Real Life** You need to find an object that has only flat surfaces for a scavenger hunt. Circle the objects you can use.

13.7 Describe Three-Dimensional Shapes

Circle the attributes of the shape.

13. **Rectangular Prism**

    6 flat surfaces

    12 vertices

    12 edges

    two-dimensional

14. **Sphere**

    0 flat surfaces

    1 flat surface

    0 edges

    rolls

13.8 Combine Three-Dimensional Shapes

15. Circle the new shape that you can make.

13.9 Take Apart Three-Dimensional Shapes

16. Circle the shapes that make up the structure.

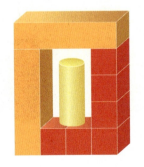   

14 Equal Shares

- What is your favorite food?
- How can you cut a sandwich so the pieces are the same size?

Chapter Learning Target:
Understand equal shares.

Chapter Success Criteria:
- I can identify shapes that show equal shares.
- I can explain which shapes are equal.
- I can compare shares.
- I can draw to show shares.

14 Vocabulary

Name _____

Review Words
bar graph
picture graph

Organize It

Use the review words to complete the graphic organizer.

☐ _____   ☐ _____

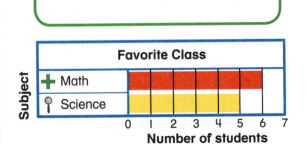

Define It

Use your vocabulary cards to complete the puzzle.

Across

1.

Down

2.   3.

674 six hundred seventy-four

Chapter 14 Vocabulary Cards

equal shares	fourth of
fourths	half of
halves	quarter of
quarters	unequal shares

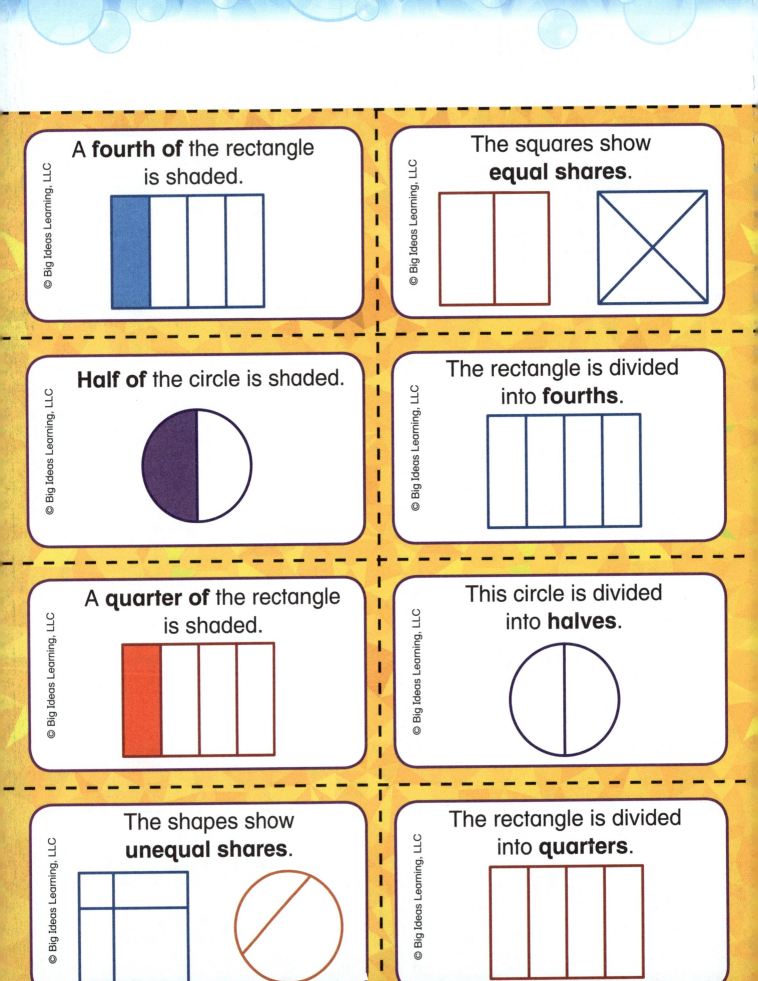

Name _____

Equal Shares

Learning Target: Identify equal shares in two-dimensional shapes.

Sort the Equal Shares Sort Cards.

Equal Parts	Unequal Parts

MP Justify a Result
How do you know which cards show equal parts?

Chapter 14 | Lesson 1   six hundred seventy-five   675

Think and Grow

Circle the shape that shows equal shares.

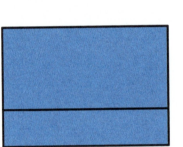

The parts are the same size. So, the rectangle shows equal parts, or **equal shares**.

The parts are not the same size. So, the rectangle shows unequal parts, or **unequal shares**.

Show and Grow — I can do it!

Circle the shape that shows equal shares.

1.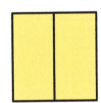

2.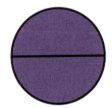

3.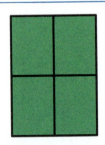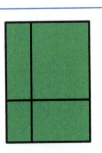

4.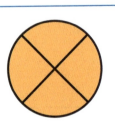

676 six hundred seventy-six

Name _____

✓ Apply and Grow: Practice

Circle the shape that shows equal shares.

5.

6.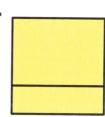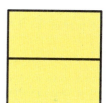

7.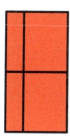

8.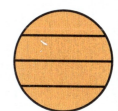

9.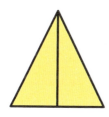

_____ equal shares

10.

_____ equal shares

11. 🍎 **YOU BE THE TEACHER** Newton says the shape shows equal shares. Is he correct? Explain.

_____

_____

Chapter 14 | Lesson 1   six hundred seventy-seven   **677**

Think and Grow: Modeling Real Life

You and your friend each design a kite. Your kite has 2 equal shares. Your friend's has 2 unequal shares. Draw to show the parts.

You

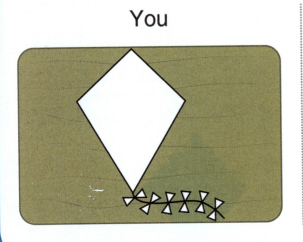

Friend

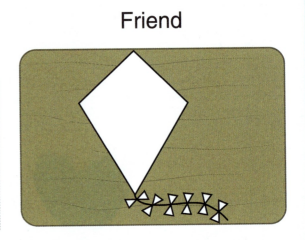

Show and Grow I can think deeper!

12. You and your friend each design a poster. Your poster has 4 unequal shares. Your friend's has 4 equal shares. Draw to show the parts.

You

Friend

678 six hundred seventy-eight

Name _____

Practice

Learning Target: Identify equal shares in two-dimensional shapes.

Equal Shares   Unequal Shares

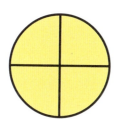 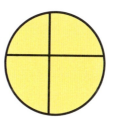 

Circle the shape that shows equal shares.

1.

2.

3.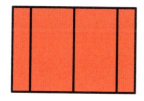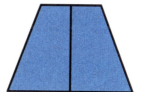

4.

5.

_____ equal shares

6.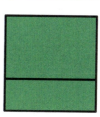

_____ equal shares

Chapter 14 | Lesson 1   six hundred seventy-nine   679

7. **Precision** Descartes makes a thank you card with 4 equal shares. Which card does Descartes make?

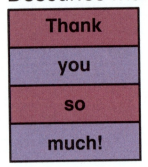 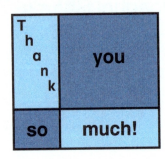

8. **DIG DEEPER!** Draw to show 4 equal shares in three different ways.

9. **Modeling Real Life** You and your friend each design a sticker. Your sticker has 2 unequal shares. Your friend's has 2 equal shares. Draw to show the parts.

You

Friend

 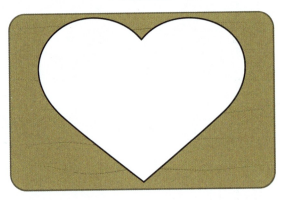

Review & Refresh

Make quick sketches to find the sum.

10. 32
   + 25

Tens	Ones

11. 61
   + 15

Tens	Ones

Name _____

Learning Target: Identify shapes that show halves.

Partition Shapes into Halves

Build hexagons with the pattern blocks shown. Circle the hexagon that shows 2 equal shares.

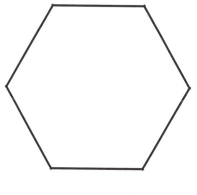
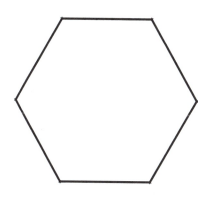

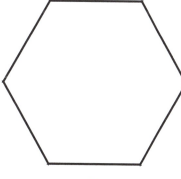

Repeated Reasoning
To show 2 equal shares, how many pattern blocks will you use?

Chapter 14 | Lesson 2

six hundred eighty-one 681

Think and Grow

Circle the shape that shows halves.

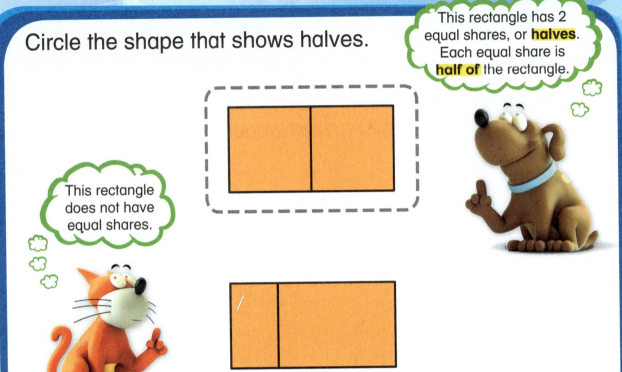

Show and Grow — I can do it!

Circle the shape that shows halves.

1.

2.

3.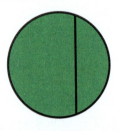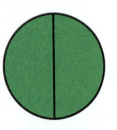

4.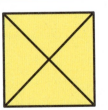

Name _____

 Apply and Grow: Practice

Circle the shapes that show halves.

5.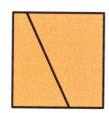

6.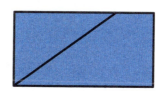

Color half of the shape.

7.    8.    9.

10. **Structure** Match each half with its whole.

Half	Whole

	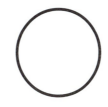

Use Math Tools
How can you use paper shapes to check your work?

Chapter 14 | Lesson 2   six hundred eighty-three   683

Think and Grow: Modeling Real Life

Show three ways to cut the cheese in half.

Check Your Work
If you cut along the lines you drew, what should be true about the shapes?

Show and Grow I can think deeper!

11. Show three ways to fold the rug in half.

Name _____

Practice 14.2

Learning Target: Identify shapes that show halves.

Circle the shape that shows halves.

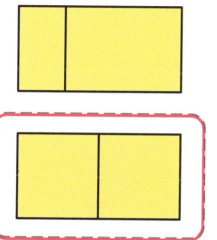

This rectangle has 2 equal shares, or **halves**. Each equal share is **half of** the rectangle.

Circle the shape that shows halves.

1.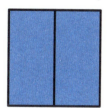

2.

Circle the shapes that show halves.

3.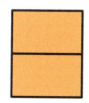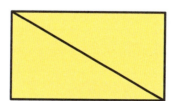

4.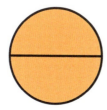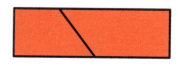

Chapter 14 | Lesson 2   six hundred eighty-five   685

Color half of the shape.

5.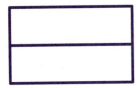

6.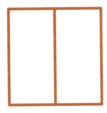

7.

8. **DIG DEEPER!** Circle the shapes that show halves.

9. **Modeling Real Life** Show three ways to fold the bandana in half.

Review & Refresh

10. Circle the shapes that only have a curved surface.

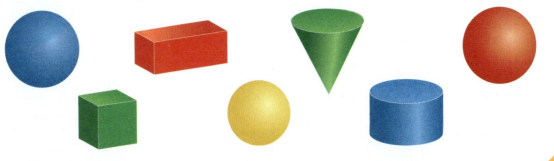

Name _____

Learning Target: Identify shapes that show fourths.

Partition Shapes into Fourths

14.3

Explore and Grow

Sort the 2, 4, or Unequal Shares Sort Cards.

2 Equal Shares
4 Equal Shares
Unequal Shares

Chapter 14 | Lesson 3

six hundred eighty-seven 687

Think and Grow

Circle the shape that shows fourths.

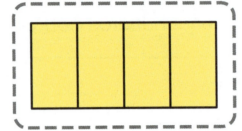

This rectangle has 4 equal shares. The equal shares are called **fourths**, or **quarters**. Each equal share is a **fourth of**, or a **quarter of** the rectangle.

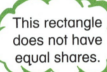

This rectangle does not have equal shares.

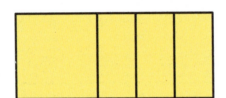

Show and Grow   I can do it!

Circle the shape that shows fourths.

1.

2.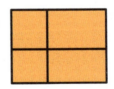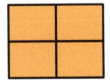

3.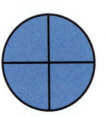

4.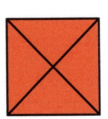

Name _____

 Apply and Grow: Practice

Circle the shapes that show fourths.

5.

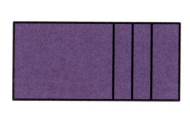   

Color a quarter of the shape.

6.  **7.**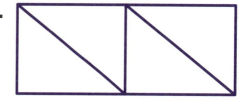

8. **Precision** Draw more lines to show fourths.

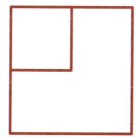

9. **DIG DEEPER!** You cut a circle into halves. Your friend cuts the same-sized circle into quarters. Who has the larger pieces? Think: How do you know?

You   Friend

Chapter 14 | Lesson 3   six hundred eighty-nine   689

Think and Grow: Modeling Real Life

You cut a pizza into quarters. Your friend eats 1 quarter. How many more friends could have a piece of pizza?

_____ friends

Show and Grow — I can think deeper!

10. You cut a granola bar into quarters. Your friend eats 2 quarters. How many more friends could have a piece of the granola bar?

_____ friends

Name _____

Practice

Learning Target: Identify shapes that show fourths.

Circle the shape that shows fourths.

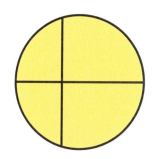 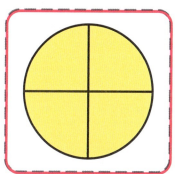

This circle has 4 equal shares. The equal shares are called fourths, or quarters.

Circle the shape that shows fourths.

1.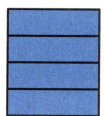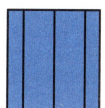

2.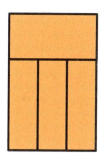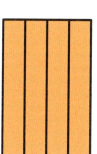

Circle the shapes that show fourths.

3.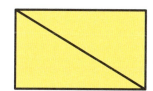

Color a quarter of the shape.

4.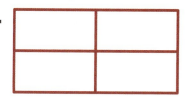

5.

Chapter 14 | Lesson 3

six hundred ninety-one

6. **DIG DEEPER!** Which shape shows a fourth of a square?

7. **Reasoning** Color half of the square. How many fourths did you color?

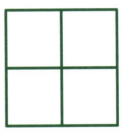

_____ fourths

8. **Modeling Real Life** You cut a slice of bread into quarters. Your friend eats 3 quarters. How many more friends could have a piece of bread?

_____ friend

Review & Refresh

Draw to show the time.

9.

10.

Name _____

Performance Task 14

1. You, your friend, and your cousin are having a picnic. Use the clues to match each person with a food item.
   - You bring an item that is cut into 4 unequal shares.
   - Your friend brings an item that is cut into halves.
   - Your cousin brings an item that is cut into quarters.

   You   Friend   Cousin

      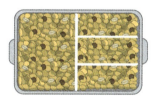

2. a. You cut an apple into 2 equal shares. You cut each share in half. How many equal shares do you have now?

   _____ equal shares

   Show how you know:

   b. You give your friend a fourth of the apple. How many shares do you have left?

   _____ shares

Chapter 14   six hundred ninety-three   693

Three In a Row: Equal Shares

To Play: Players take turns. On your turn, spin the spinner. Cover a square that matches your spin. Continue playing until a player gets three in a row.

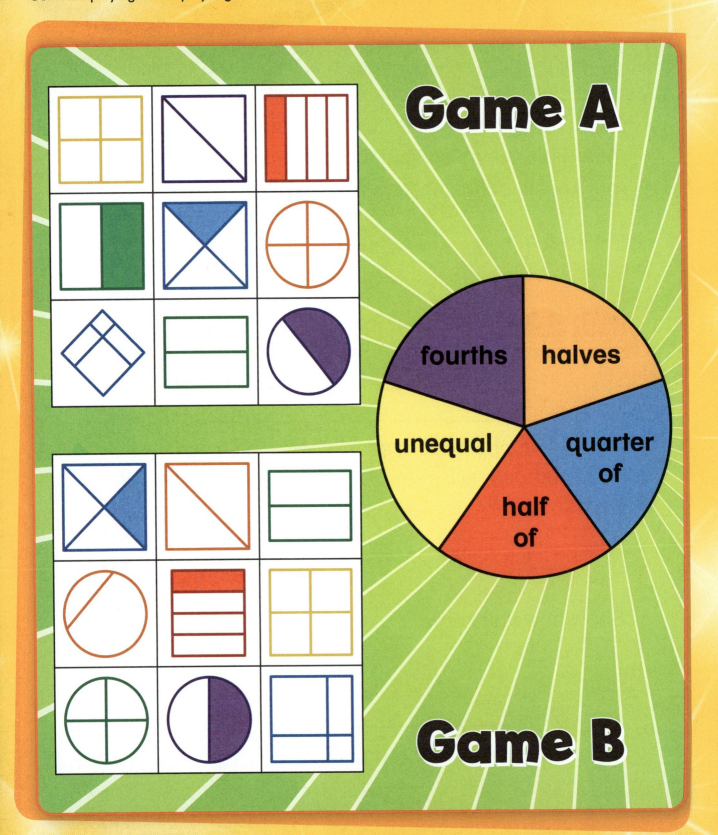

Name _____

Chapter Practice 14

14.1 Equal Shares

1.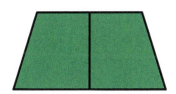

   _____ equal shares

2.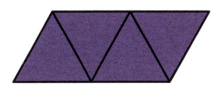

   _____ equal shares

3. **Modeling Real Life** Newton and Descartes each design a place mat. Newton's has 4 equal shares. Descartes's has 4 unequal shares. Draw to show the parts.

   Newton
   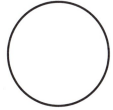

   Descartes
   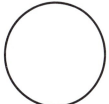

14.2 Partition Shapes into Halves

4. Circle the shapes that show halves.

   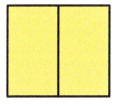   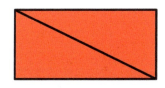

5. **Structure** Match each half with its whole.

Half   Whole

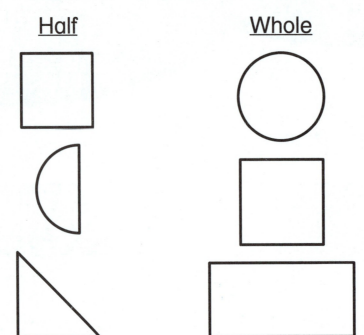

 Partition Shapes into Fourths

6. Circle the shapes that show fourths.

Color a quarter of the shape.

7.

8.

Name _____

Cumulative Practice 1-14

1. Shade the circle next to the equation that tells how many fewer students chose manga comics than superhero comics.

Favorite Comics	
Science Fiction	卌
Superhero	卌 III
Manga	II

○ $5 + 8 + 2 = 15$

○ $8 - 5 = 3$

○ $8 + 2 = 10$

○ $8 - 2 = 6$

2. Shade the circle next to the number that tells how many minutes are in a half hour.

○ 15 ○ 30 ○ 45 ○ 60

3. Shade the circle next to the shape that does *not* show fourths.

 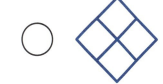

Chapter 14 — six hundred ninety-seven

4. Shade the circle next to the shape that has no straight sides.

 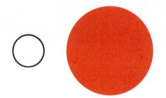

 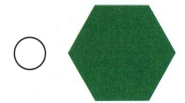

5. Shade the circle next to the difference.

17 − 8 = _____

◯ 8   ◯ 9
◯ 10 ◯ 12

6. Draw lines to show halves.

7. Write the time on the clock two ways.

_____

____ : ____

8.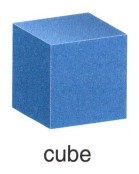

_____ flat surfaces

_____ vertices

cube

_____ edges

9. Shade the circles next to the choices that match the model.

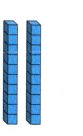 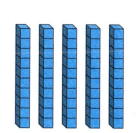

○ 7 ones

○ 2 tens + 5 tens

○ 70

○ 20 + 50

10. Shade the circles next to the choices that show the shapes you can use to make a ⬣.

○    ○

○    ○

11. Tell how many equal shares.

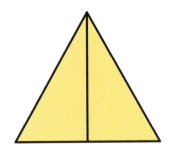 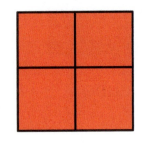

_____ equal shares   _____ equal shares

12. A group of students are at a park. 2 of them leave. There are 4 left. How many students were at the park to start?

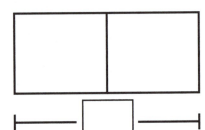

_____ − _____ = _____

_____ students

13. Circle the shapes that make up the structure.

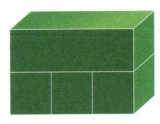

Glossary

A

add [sumar]

○ + ○○ = ○○○
○　 ○○ 　○○○

2 + 4 = 6

addend [sumando]

4 + 3 = 7

addition equation [ecuación de adición]

4 + 5 = 9

analog clock [reloj analogo]

B

bar graph [gráfica de barras]

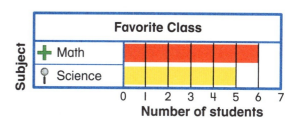

bar model [modelo de barra]

You: | 5 |

Friend: | 2 | 3 |

C

column [columna]

1	2	3	4	5	6	7	8	9	10
11	12	13	14	15	16	17	18	19	20
21	22	23	24	25	26	27	28	29	30
31	32	33	34	35	36	37	38	39	40
41	42	43	44	45	46	47	48	49	50
51	52	53	54	55	56	57	58	59	60
61	62	63	64	65	66	67	68	69	70
71	72	73	74	75	76	77	78	79	80
81	82	83	84	85	86	87	88	89	90
91	92	93	94	95	96	97	98	99	100
101	102	103	104	105	106	107	108	109	110
111	112	113	114	115	116	117	118	119	120

A1

compare [comparar]

There are more red cubes than yellow cubes.

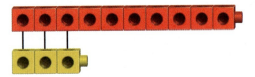

count back [contar hacia atrás]

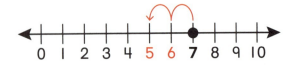

count on [contar hacia delante]

curved surface [superficie curva]

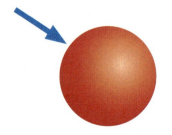

data [datos]

Favorite Class
math   science
science math
science math
math   science
math   science
math

decade numbers [números de la década]

1	2	3	4	5	6	7	8	9	10
11	12	13	14	15	16	17	18	19	20
21	22	23	24	25	26	27	28	29	30
31	32	33	34	35	36	37	38	39	40
41	42	43	44	45	46	47	48	49	50
51	52	53	54	55	56	57	58	59	60
61	62	63	64	65	66	67	68	69	70
71	72	73	74	75	76	77	78	79	80
81	82	83	84	85	86	87	88	89	90
91	92	93	94	95	96	97	98	99	100
101	102	103	104	105	106	107	108	109	110
111	112	113	114	115	116	117	118	119	120

difference [diferencia]

$$8 - 3 = 5$$

digit [dígito]

The digits of 16 are 1 and 6.

16

digital clock   [reloj digital]

doubles   [dobles]

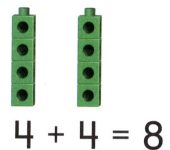

4 + 4 = 8

doubles minus 1
[dobles menos 1]

4 + 4 = 8, so 4 + 3 = 7

doubles plus 1
[dobles más 1]

4 + 4 = 8, so 4 + 5 = 9

edge   [arista]

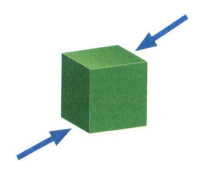

equal shares   [partes iguales]

The squares show **equal shares**.

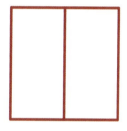 

equals   [igual]

8 + 2 = 10

8 plus 2 equals 10

A3

fact family [hecho de la familia]

2 + 3 = 5
3 + 2 = 5
5 − 2 = 3
5 − 3 = 2

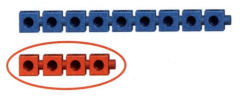

fewer [menos]

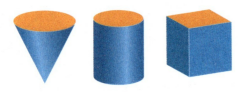

flat surface [superficie plana]

fourth of [cuarto de]

A **fourth of** the rectangle is shaded.

fourths [cuartos]

The rectangle is divided into **fourths**.

greater than [mayor que]

26 is greater than 23.

26 > 23

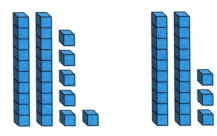

half hour [media hora]

A half hour is 30 minutes.

half of [mitad de]

Half of the circle is shaded.

half past [y media]

half past 3

halves [mitades]

This circle is divided into **halves**.

hour [hora]

An hour is 60 minutes.

hour hand [horario]

L

length [longitud]

length unit [unidad de longitud]

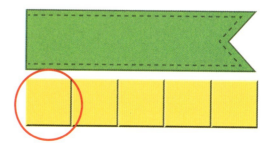

less than [menor que]

22 is less than 38.

22 < 38

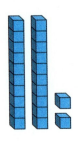 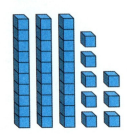

longest [más largo]

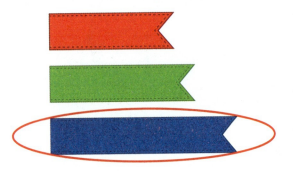

measure [medida]

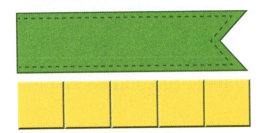

minus [menos]

3 − 1

3 minus 1

minute [minuto]

60 minutes is 1 hour.

minute hand [minutero]

more [más]

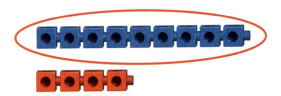

N

number line [numero de linea]

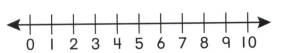

O

o'clock [en punto]

3 o'clock

---

120 chart [120 gráfico]

1	2	3	4	5	6	7	8	9	10
11	12	13	14	15	16	17	18	19	20
21	22	23	24	25	26	27	28	29	30
31	32	33	34	35	36	37	38	39	40
41	42	43	44	45	46	47	48	49	50
51	52	53	54	55	56	57	58	59	60
61	62	63	64	65	66	67	68	69	70
71	72	73	74	75	76	77	78	79	80
81	82	83	84	85	86	87	88	89	90
91	92	93	94	95	96	97	98	99	100
101	102	103	104	105	106	107	108	109	110
111	112	113	114	115	116	117	118	119	120

---

ones [unidades]

23 has 3 ones.

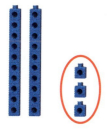

---

ones place [un lugar]

2<u>3</u>

---

open number line [abrir la línea numérica]

P

part [parte]

---

part-part-whole model [modelo parte-parte-todo]

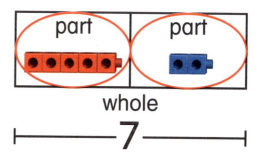

---

picture graph [gráfico de imagen]

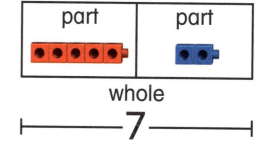

Each 🙂 = 1 student.

plus   [más]

$$2 + 1$$
$$2 \text{ plus } 1$$

quarter of   [cuarta parte de]

A **quarter of** the rectangle is shaded.

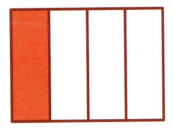

quarters   [cuartas partes]

The rectangle is divided into **quarters**.

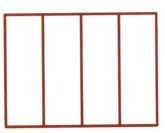

rectangular prism
[prisma rectangular]

rhombus   [rombo]

row   [fila]

1	2	3	4	5	6	7	8	9	10
11	12	13	14	15	16	17	18	19	20
21	22	23	24	25	26	27	28	29	30
31	32	33	34	35	36	37	38	39	40
41	42	43	44	45	46	47	48	49	50
51	52	53	54	55	56	57	58	59	60
61	62	63	64	65	66	67	68	69	70
71	72	73	74	75	76	77	78	79	80
81	82	83	84	85	86	87	88	89	90
91	92	93	94	95	96	97	98	99	100
101	102	103	104	105	106	107	108	109	110
111	112	113	114	115	116	117	118	119	120

S

shortest [el más corto]

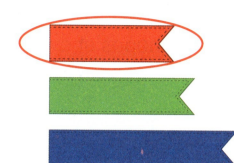

side [lado]

subtract [restar]

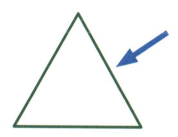

$6 - 4 = 2$

subtraction equation [ecuación de resta]

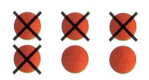

sum [suma]

$5 + 3 = 8$

T

tally chart [tabla de conteo]

Favorite Class	
Math	|||||	
Science	|||||

tally mark [marca de conteo]

Favorite Class	
Math	|||||	
Science	|||||

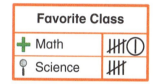

tens [decenas]

23 has 2 tens.

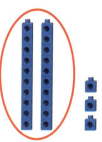

tens place [lugar de decenas]

23

three-dimensional shape
[forma tridimensional]

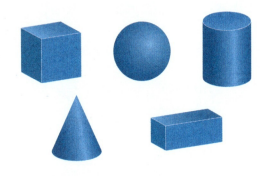

trapezoid [trapecio]

two-dimensional shape
[forma bidimensional]

unequal shares
[partes desiguales]

The shapes show **unequal shares**.

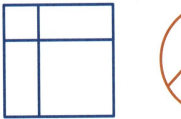 

vertex [vértice]

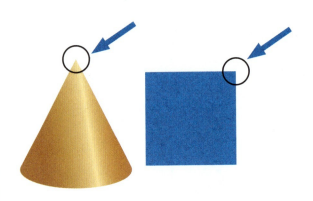

whole [todo]

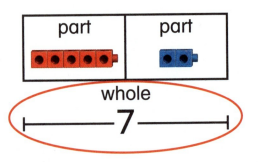

Index

Add to
   solving problems with, 3–14
      with change unknown, 45–50
      with missing addend, 45–50, 127–132
      with start unknown, 127–132
   writing equations for, 3–8
Addends, 10, *See also* Addition
   missing or unknown
      add to problems with, 45–50, 127–132
      making 10, 163–168
      part–part–whole model of, 94, 128–132
      put together problems with, 21–26, 51–56
      ten frame for finding, 100
   order of, 95–100
   same, in adding doubles, 83–88, 187–192
Addition
   of 0, 65–70
   of 1, 77–82
   in any order, 95–100
   using "count on" strategy, 101–106
      within 20, 199–204, 230
      of tens to number, 446, 449
   using doubles, 89–94
      from 1 to 5, 83–88
      from 6 to 10, 187–192
      within 20, 193–198
      with doubles minus 1 strategy, 89–94, 193–198
      with doubles plus 1 strategy, 89–94, 193–198
   using "make a 10" strategy
      adding 9 in, 217–222
      adding one-digit number to two-digit number in, 471–476
      adding three numbers in, 211–216
      adding two numbers in, 223–228
      adding two-digit numbers in, 482
      finding addends in, 163–168
   using part–part–whole model, 16–20
   using place value, 477–482
   practicing strategies of, 483–488
   solving problems using, 489–494
      within 20, 229–234
      add to, 3–14
      add to, with change unknown, 45–50
      add to, with missing addend, 45–50, 127–132
      add to, with start unknown, 127–132
      bigger unknown, 145–150
      put together, 15–20
      put together, connected with take apart, 51–56
      put together, missing both addends, 21–26
   of tens, 415–420
      using mental math, 403–408
      to number, 445–450
      on number line, 421–426, 446, 449
   of tens and ones, 459–464
      on number line, 465–470, 484, 490, 493
   of three numbers, 205–216
Addition equations, *See also* Addition
   add to, 3–14, 45–50
   completing fact families with, 169–174, 520
   definition of, 4
   put together, 15–26
   true or false, 157–162, 267–272, 372, 482
   writing, 3–8
Addition sentence, 4 (*See also* Addition equations)
Addition to subtract strategy, 113–118
   within 20, 249–254
   of tens, 439–444
All, subtracting, 71–76

A11

Analog clock
    definition of, 584
    using hour and minute hand of, 595–600
    using hour hand of
        to tell time to half hour, 589–594
        to tell time to hour, 583–588
    using to tell time, 601–606

Another Way, 200, 446, 449, 466, 484, 487

Apply and Grow: Practice, *In every lesson. For example, see:* 5, 67, 129, 189, 245, 295, 357, 405, 461, 505

B

Bar graphs
    definition of, 554
    making, 559–564
    picture graphs compared to, 553
    reading and interpreting, 553–558
    solving problems with data from, 565–570

Bar model
    adding within 20 using, 231, 232, 234
    compare problems using
        with bigger unknown, 146–150
        with length measurement, 528–532
        with smaller unknown, 152–156
    definition of, 146
    subtraction using, within 20, 281, 282

Bigger unknown, compare problems with, 145–150

C

Challenge, *See* Dig Deeper

Change, unknown
    add to problems with, 45–50
    take from problems with, 133–138

Chapter Practice, *In every chapter. For example, see:* 59–62, 121–124, 177–180, 237–240, 287–290, 349–352, 393–396, 453–456, 497–500, 535–538

Charts
    120
        for counting by ones, 293–298
        for counting by tens, 299–304
        definition of, 694
    hundred
        for adding 10, 404, 406
        for adding tens and ones, 465–470
        for subtracting 10, 410, 413
    tally
        completing picture and bar graphs with, 559–564
        definition of, 542
        making, 541–546, 559
        picture graphs compared to, 547
        solving problems with data from, 565–570

Choose Tools, 627, 630

Circles
    combining shapes to make, 626, 632
    describing, 619, 621
    as flat surfaces, of shapes, 644–648
    identifying equal shares in, 676, 677, 679
        fourths, 688–692
        halves, 682–686
    taking apart, 639

Clock
    analog and digital, 601–606
    using hour and minute hands of, 595–600
    using hour hand of
        to tell time to half hour, 589–594
        to tell time to hour, 583–588

Closed shapes
    definition of, 614
    sorting, 614–618

Color tiles
    comparing length using, 528–532
    measuring length using, 516–526
    representing data with, 559–564

Columns, in 120 chart, 300

Combining shapes
    three-dimensional, 655–660
    two-dimensional, 625–636

Common Errors, *Throughout. For example, see:* T-22, 199
Common Misconceptions, *Throughout. For example, see:* T-22, T-40, T-102, T-128, T-148
Compare, definition of, 356
Compare problems, solving
    bigger unknown, 145–150
    how many fewer, 39–44, 151–156
    how many more, 33–38, 145–150
    length, 527–532
    smaller unknown, 151–156
Comparing length
    indirectly, using third object, 509–514
    ordering objects by length, 503–508
    solving compare problems, 527–532
Comparing numbers
    1 more, 1 less, 385–390
    10 more, 10 less, 385–390
    11 to 19, 355–360
    within 100, 361–366
        using number line, 379–384
        using place value, 367–372
        using symbols, 373–378
    quick sketches for, 357, 359, 365, 373–375, 444
Composing numbers
    11 to 19, 305–310
    to 120, 341–346
    counting by tens and ones for, 317–322
    decade numbers (tens), 311–316
    in different ways, 335–340
    quick sketches for, 323–328, 360
    understanding place value in, 329–334
Cones
    combining with other shapes, 655–657, 659
    definition of, 650
    describing, 649–654
    taking apart shapes containing, 661–666
"Count back" strategy
    definition of, 108
    subtraction using, 107–112, 434, 437
    within 20, 243–248, 280
"Count on" strategy
    addition using, 101–106
        within 20, 199–204, 230
        of tens to number, 446, 449
    definition of, 102
    subtraction using, 250–254, 440, 443
Counting
    to 120 by ones, 293–298
    to 120 by tens, 299–304
    to add 1, 78
    tens and ones, to write numbers, 317–322
Cross-Curricular Connections, *In every lesson. For example, see:* T-13, T-161, T-197, T-365, T-419, T-487, T-525, T-563, T-605, T-685
Cubes
    combining, to make new shapes, 655–660
    definition of, 650
    describing, 649–654
    taking apart shapes containing, 661–666
Cumulative Practice, 181–184, 397–400, 577–580, 697–700
Curved surfaces
    definition of, 644
    sorting shapes by, 644–648
Cylinders
    combining with other shapes, 655–657, 659
    definition of, 650
    describing, 649–654
    taking apart shapes containing, 661–666

D

Data
    bar graphs of
        definition of, 554
        making, 559–564
        picture graphs compared to, 553
        reading and interpreting, 553–558

solving problems with data from, 565–570
definition of, 542
picture graphs of
bar graphs compared to, 553
definition of, 543
making, 559–564
reading and interpreting, 547–552
solving problems with data from, 565–570
tally charts compared to, 547
representing, 559–564
solving problems involving, 565–570
tally charts of, 541–546
completing picture and bar graphs with, 559–564
definition of, 542
making, 541–546, 559
picture graphs compared to, 547
solving problems with data from, 565–570

Decade numbers, 300, 311–316 (See also Tens (10))

Decomposing
take apart problems, 52–56
taking apart shapes
three-dimensional, 661–666
two-dimensional, 637–642

Define It, *In every chapter. For example, see:* 2, 64, 126, 186, 242, 292, 354, 402, 458, 502

Differences, 28 (See also Subtraction)

Differentiation, See Scaffolding Instruction

Dig Deeper, *Throughout. For example, see:* 5, 67, 195, 245, 304, 357, 405, 482, 508, 555

Digit(s)
comparing in two-digit numbers, 367–372
definition of, 330
value in two-digit number, 329–334

Digital clock
definition of, 602
telling time on, 601–606

Doubles
using
within 20, 193–198
to find sum, 89–94, 193–198
adding
from 1 to 5, 83–88
from 6 to 10, 187–192
within 20, 193–198
with doubles minus 1 strategy, 89–94, 193–198
with doubles plus 1 strategy, 89–94, 193–198
definition of, 84

Doubles minus 1, 89–94, 193–198

Doubles plus 1, 89–94, 193–198

E

Edges, of three-dimensional shapes, 650–654

ELL Support, *In every lesson. For example, see:* T-2, T-127, T-235, T-282, T-312, T-385, T-430, T-465, T-586, T-682

Equal shares
definition of, 676
identifying, 675–680
shapes showing fourths, 687–692
shapes showing halves, 681–686

Equals (equal to), 10, 373–378

Equations
addition
add to, 3–14
completing fact families with, 169–174, 520
definition of, 4
put together, 15–26
true or false, 157–162, 267–272, 372, 482
writing, 3–8
subtraction
completing fact families with, 169–174, 520

how many fewer, 40–44
how many more, 34–38
take apart, 52–56
take from, 27–32
true or false, 157–162, 267–272, 372, 482
writing, 28–32
true, finding number making, 273–278

Error Analysis, *See* You Be the Teacher

Explain, *Throughout. For example, see:* 411, 450, 485, 505, 523, 541, 570, 600, 613, 686

Explore and Grow, *In every lesson. For example, see:* 3, 65, 127, 187, 243, 293, 355, 403, 459, 541

F

Fact families
completing, 169–174, 520
definition of, 170

Fewer
1 or 10, identifying numbers with, 385–390
definition of, 40
how many, compare problems solving for, 39–44, 151–156

Flat surfaces
definition of, 644
describing shapes by, 649–654
sorting shapes by, 644–648

Formative Assessment, *Throughout. For example, see:* T-6, T-74, T-202, T-276, T-344, T-406, T-556, T-604, T-646, T-678

Fourth of, 688

Fourths
definition of, 688
identifying shapes showing, 687–692

G

Games, *In every chapter. For example, see:* 58, 120, 176, 236, 286, 348, 392, 452, 496, 534

"Get to 10" strategy, subtraction using, 261–266, 426
subtracting nine in, 255–260

Graphs
bar
definition of, 554
making, 559–564
picture graphs compared to, 553
reading and interpreting, 553–558
solving problems with data from, 565–570
picture
bar graphs compared to, 553
definition of, 543
making, 559–564
reading and interpreting, 547–552
solving problems with data from, 565–570
tally charts compared to, 547

Greater than (>), 356, 373–378 (*See also* Comparing numbers)

Groups of objects, *See also specific operations and problems*
adding to, 3–14
compare problems
how many fewer, 39–44
how many more, 33–38
putting together, 15–26
taking apart, 51–56
taking from, 27–32

H

Half of, 682, 685

Half hour
on analog and digital clocks, 601–606
definition of, 590

telling time to
hour and minute hands for, 595–600
hour hand for, 589–594

Half past
on analog and digital clocks, 601–606
definition of, 590
hour and minute hands showing, 595–600
hour hand showing, 589–594

Halves
definition of, 682
identifying shapes showing, 681–686

Hexagons
combining, to make new shapes, 628, 631
combining shapes to make, 626–629
definition of, 620
describing, 619–624
equal shares in, identifying, 677, 681
halves of, 681
taking apart, 639, 642

Higher Order Thinking, *See* Dig Deeper

Hour
on analog and digital clocks, 601–606
definition of, 584
telling time to
hour and minute hands for, 595–600
hour hand for, 583–588

Hour hand
definition of, 584
using to tell time to half hour, 589–594
using to tell time to hour, 583–588
using to tell time to hour and half hour, 595–600

Hundred chart
for adding 10, 404, 406
for adding tens and ones, 465–470
for subtracting 10, 410, 413

L

Learning Target, *In every lesson. For example, see:* 3, 65, 127, 187, 243, 293, 355, 459, 503, 541

Length
comparing indirectly, 509–514
measuring
using color tiles, 516–526
using like objects, 515–520
using paper clips, 521–526
ordering objects by, 503–508
solving compare problems involving, 527–532

Length unit
color tiles of, 516–520
definition of, 516

Less than (<), 356, 373–378 (*See also* Comparing numbers)

Linking cubes
for add to problems, 3, 9, 10, 13
for adding 0, 65
for adding 1, 77
for adding doubles, 84–88, 90, 188, 189, 191
for adding in any order, 96, 97, 99
for adding three numbers, 205
for adding within 20, 233
for completing fact families, 169
for composing numbers
11 to 19, 306, 309
decade numbers (tens), 312–316
for doubles minus 1 strategy, 90, 91, 93, 194, 195, 197
for doubles plus 1 strategy, 90, 91, 93, 194, 195, 197
for grouping by 10, 312–316
for put together problems, 21
for take from problems, 27, 28, 31

Logic, 67, 70, 473, 476

Longest
definition of, 504
ordering objects by, 503–508

L-shaped vertices, 615, 616, 619, 622

"Make a 10" strategy, addition using
　adding 9 in, 217–222
　adding one-digit number to two-digit number in, 471–476
　adding three numbers in, 211–216
　adding two numbers in, 223–228
　adding two-digit numbers in, 482
　finding addends in, 163–168

Mathematical Practices
　Make sense of problems and persevere in solving them, *Throughout. For example, see:* 40, 119, 144, 226, 272, 388, 406, 565, 684
　Reason abstractly and quantitatively, *Throughout. For example, see:* 17, 122, 174, 225, 310, 461, 606, 639, 692
　Construct viable arguments and critique the reasoning of others, *Throughout. For example, see:* 21, 118, 231, 335, 355, 414, 476, 613, 675
　Model with mathematics, *Throughout. For example, see:* 112, 168, 192, 234, 264, 334, 518, 571, 622
　Use appropriate tools strategically, *Throughout. For example, see:* 4, 109, 163, 190, 270, 334, 438, 509, 563
　Attend to precision, *Throughout. For example, see:* 12, 114, 150, 204, 295, 372, 414, 503, 689
　Look for and make use of structure, *Throughout. For example, see:* 50, 178, 201, 301, 385, 441, 527, 583, 683
　Look for and express regularity in repeated reasoning, *Throughout. For example, see:* 34, 78, 135, 219, 249, 311, 379, 433, 681

Mental math
　adding 10 using, 403–408
　subtracting 10 using, 409–414

Minus (−), 28

Minute
　on analog and digital clocks, 601–606
　definition of, 596
　telling time to, 595–600

Minute hand
　definition of, 596
　using to tell time to hour and half hour, 595–600

Missing addends
　add to problems with, 45–50, 127–132
　making 10, 163–168
　part–part–whole model of, 94, 128–132
　put together problems with, 21–26, 51–56
　ten frame for finding, 100

Modeling, of numbers, *See also* Bar model; Part–part–whole model
　in different ways, 335–340
　as tens and ones, 323–328, 360
　two-digit, 329–334

Modeling Real Life, *In every lesson. For example, see:* 8, 70, 132, 192, 248, 304, 360, 408, 464, 508

More
　1 or 10, identifying numbers with, 385–390
　definition of, 34
　how many, compare problems solving for, 33–38, 145–150

Multiple Representations, *Throughout. For example, see:* 4, 103, 170, 218, 260, 306, 351, 446, 547, 692

Nine (9)
　adding, using "make a 10" strategy, 217–222
　subtracting, in "get to 10" strategy, 255–260

A17

Number line
- adding on
    - within 20, 199–204
    - using "count on" strategy, 101–106, 199–204, 230, 446, 449
    - solving word problems with, 230, 234
    - of tens, 421–426, 446, 449
    - of tens and ones, 465–470, 484, 490, 493
- comparing numbers on, 379–384
- definition of, 102
- finding number making true equation on, 273
- open, definition of, 422
- subtracting on
    - within 20, 243–254, 280
    - using addition to subtract strategy, 249–254
    - using "count back" strategy, 107–112, 243–248, 280
    - using "count on" strategy, 250–254, 440, 443
    - of tens, 433–438

Number Sense, *Throughout. For example, see:* 17, 20, 91, 94, 97, 100, 123, 159, 225, 263, 307, 366, 387, 390

O

120
- counting to, 341–346
    - by ones, 293–298
    - by tens, 299–304
- writing numbers to, 341–346

120 chart
- for counting by ones, 293–298
- for counting by tens, 299–304
- definition of, 294

Objects, groups of, *See also* specific operations and problems
- adding to, 3–14
- compare problems
    - how many fewer, 39–44
    - how many more, 33–38
- putting together, 15–26
- taking apart, 51–56
- taking from, 27–32

O'clock
- on analog and digital clocks, 601–606
- to half hour, 589–594
- to hour, 583–588
- to hour and half hour, 595–600

Ones (1)
- adding, 77–82
    - in adding tens to number, 445–450
    - in adding two numbers, with tens, 459–470
    - in adding two-digit numbers, 477–482
    - on number line, 465–470, 484, 490, 493
    - one-digit numbers to two-digit number, 471–476
- in comparing numbers
    - 1 more, 1 less, 385–390
    - 11 to 19, 355–360
    - within 100, 361–372, 374
- in composing or writing numbers
    - 11 to 19, 305–310
    - to 120, 341–346
    - counting for, 317–322
    - in different ways, 335–340
    - quick sketches for, 323–328, 360
    - in two-digit number, 329–334
- counting to 120 by, 293–298
- definition of, 306
- subtracting, 77–82

Ones place, 306, 329–334

Open number line, *See also* Number line
- definition of, 422

Open shapes
- definition of, 614
- sorting, 614–618

Organize It, *In every chapter. For example, see:* 2, 64, 126, 186, 242, 292, 354, 402, 612, 674

P

Paper clips
    comparing length using, 528–532
    measuring length using, 521–526

Part, definition of, 16

Partitioning shapes
    into equal shares, 675–680
    into fourths, 687–692
    into halves, 681–686

Part–part–whole model
    add to using, 46–50, 128–132
    adding within 20 using, 233
    addition to subtract strategy using, 114–118
    completing fact families using, 170, 171, 173
    definition of, 16
    finding missing addend in, 94, 128–132
    put together using, 16–20
    put together/take apart using, 52–56
    subtracting within 20 using, 281, 283, 284
    take from problems using
        with change unknown, 134–138
        with start unknown, 140–144

Performance Task, *In every chapter. For example, see:* 57, 119, 175, 235, 285, 347, 391, 451, 495, 533, 571, 607, 667, 693

Picture graphs
    bar graphs compared to, 553
    definition of, 543
    making, 559–564
    reading and interpreting, 547–552
    solving problems with data from, 565–570
    tally charts compared to, 547

Place value
    in addition of two-digit numbers, 477–482
    in comparing numbers
        11 to 19, 355–360
        within 100, 367–372
    in composing or writing numbers
        11 to 19, 305–310
        to 120, 341–346
        counting tens and ones for, 317–322
        decade numbers (tens), 311–316
        in different ways, 335–340
        quick sketches for, 323–328, 360
        in two-digit numbers, 329–334
    understanding, 329–334

Plus sign (+), 10

Practice, *In every lesson. For example, see:* 7–8, 69–70, 131–132, 191–192, 247–248, 297–298, 359–360, 407–408, 463–464, 507–508

Precision, *Throughout. For example, see:* 29, 147, 369, 372, 517, 585, 588, 621, 624, 680

Prisms, rectangular
    combining, to make new shapes, 655–657, 659
    definition of, 650
    describing, 649–654
    taking apart shapes containing, 661–666

Problem solving, *See* Word problems

Problem Solving Strategy, *Throughout. For example, see:* 230, 233, 282, 490, 492

Problem Types, *Throughout. For example, see:*
    add to
        change unknown, 45, 106, 168, 233, 400, 491
        result unknown, 4, 65, 162, 199, 228, 272, 408, 426, 450, 564
        start unknown, 130, 132, 233
    compare
        bigger unknown, 146, 178, 204, 232, 240, 470, 486, 500
        difference unknown, 34, 119, 180, 246, 285, 451, 528, 576, 658, 697
        smaller unknown, 152, 179, 196, 264, 283, 432, 493, 530, 594
    put together
        addend unknown, 98, 100, 175, 183, 562

both addends unknown, 22, 57, 60, 86, 192
total unknown, 16, 52, 119, 187, 205, 235, 418, 462, 480, 579
take apart
addend unknown, 116, 175, 183, 562
both addends unknown, 57, 397
total unknown, 52, 55, 62, 119, 258
take from
change unknown, 136, 138, 252, 279, 290
result unknown, 28, 71, 112, 243, 412, 436, 451, 526, 567, 578
start unknown, 142, 281, 290, 398, 700
Put together problems, solving, 15–20
connected with take apart, 51–56
missing both addends, 21–26

Q

Quarters
definition of, 688
identifying, 687–692
Quick sketches
for adding tens to number, 446, 449
for comparing numbers, 357, 359, 365, 373–375, 444
for modeling numbers as tens and ones, 323–328, 360
for modeling two-digit numbers, 329–334

R

Reading, *Throughout. For example, see:* T-7, T-87, T-155, T-247, T-297, T-425, T-513, T-551, T-587, T-679
Real World, *See* Modeling Real Life
Reasoning, *Throughout. For example, see:* 122, 153, 189, 461, 520, 543, 624, 639, 642, 692
Rectangles
combining, to make squares, 632
combining shapes to make, 626, 627, 633

definition of, 620
describing, 619–624
equal shares in, identifying, 676, 677, 679, 680
fourths, 688–692
halves, 682–686
as flat surfaces, of shapes, 644–648
taking apart shapes containing, 637–642
Rectangular prisms
combining, to make new shapes, 655–657, 659
definition of, 650
describing, 649–654
taking apart shapes containing, 661–666
Repeated Reasoning, 135
Response to Intervention, *Throughout. For example, see:* T-1B, T-115, T-137, T-201, T-241B, T-333, T-443, T-539B, T-587, T-615
Review & Refresh, *In every lesson. For example, see:* 8, 76, 210, 278, 372, 444, 514, 588, 624, 692
Rhombus
combining shapes to make, 627, 628, 633, 635
definition of, 620
describing, 619–624
Rows
in 120 chart, 293–294
in hundred chart, 404, 406, 410, 413

S

Scaffolding Instruction, *In every lesson. For example, see:* T-5, T-147, T-231, T-337, T-369, T-411, T-505, T-555, T-645, T-689
Shapes, *See also specific shapes*
three-dimensional
combining to make new shapes, 655–660
curved surfaces of, 644–648
describing, 649–654

edges of, 650–654
flat surfaces of, 644–654
sorting, 643–648
taking apart, 661–666
vertices of, 649–654
two-dimensional
closed or open, 614–618
combining to make new shapes, 625–636
definition of, 614
describing, 619–624
equal shares in, fourths, 687–692
equal shares in, halves, 681–686
equal shares in, identifying, 675–680
number of sides, 614–624
number of vertices, 614–624
sorting, 613–618
taking apart, 637–642

Shortest
definition of, 504
ordering objects by, 503–508

Show and Grow, *In every lesson. For example, see:* 4, 66, 128, 188, 244, 294, 356, 404, 460, 504

Show how you know, *Throughout. For example, see:* 24, 295, 208, 235, 278, 301, 349, 588

Sides, of two-dimensional shapes
definition of, 614
describing, 619–624
sorting by number of, 614–618

Smaller unknown, compare problems with, 151–156

Spheres
combining with other shapes, 655
definition of, 650
describing, 649–654
taking apart shapes containing, 661

Squares
combining, to make new shapes, 627, 635
combining shapes to make, 632
definition of, 620
describing, 619–624

equal shares in, identifying, 676, 677, 679, 680
fourths, 688, 689, 691, 692
halves, 682, 683, 685, 686
as flat surfaces, of shapes, 644–648
taking apart shapes containing, 637–642

Start, unknown
add to problems with, 127–132
take from problems with, 139–144

Straight sides, of two-dimensional shapes
describing, 619–624
number of, 614–618

Structure, *Throughout. For example, see:* 47, 50, 53, 73, 109, 129, 141, 171, 201, 260, 295, 384, 423, 467, 683

Subtraction
of 0 or all, 71–76
of 1, 77–82
using addition to subtract strategy, 113–118
within 20, 249–254
of tens, 439–444
using bar model, within 20, 281, 282
using "count back" strategy, 107–112, 434, 437
within 20, 243–248, 280
using "count on" strategy, 250–254, 440, 443
definition of, 28
using "get to 10" strategy, 261–266, 426
subtracting 9 in, 255–260
solving problems using
within 20, 279–284
how many fewer, 39–44, 151–156
how many more, 34–38
smaller unknown, 151–156
take apart, connected with put together, 51–56
take from, 27–32
take from, with change unknown, 133–138
take from, with start unknown, 139–144

A21

of tens, 427–432
    using addition to subtract strategy, 439–444
    using mental math, 409–414
    on number line, 433–438
Subtraction equations, *See also* Subtraction
    completing fact families with, 169–174, 520
    how many fewer, 40–44
    how many more, 34–38
    take apart, 52–56
    take from, 27–32
    true or false, 157–162, 267–272, 372, 482
    writing, 28–32
Success Criteria, *In every lesson. For example, see:* T-3, T-71, T-139, T-267, T-323, T-445, T-521, T-583, T-661, T-687
Sums, 10 (*See also* Addition)
    adding zero (0) and, 66
    given, finding unknown addends for, 21–26
Surfaces, 644–648
    describing shapes by, 649–654
    sorting shapes by, 643–648
Symbols
    equal to (=), 10, 373–378
    greater than (>), 356, 373–378
    less than (<), 356, 373–378
    minus sign (−), 28
    plus sign (+), 10

T

Take apart problems, 52–56
Take from problems, solving, 27–32
    with change unknown, 133–138
    with start unknown, 139–144
Taking apart shapes
    three-dimensional, 661–666
    two-dimensional, 637–642
Tally charts
    completing picture and bar graphs with, 559–564
    definition of, 542
    making, 541–546, 559
    picture graphs compared to, 547
    solving problems with data from, 565–570
Tally mark, 542 (*See also* Tally charts)
Ten frames
    for composing numbers, 305, 307, 310
    for finding missing addend, 100
    for "get to 10" strategy, 261–266, 426
        in subtracting 9, 255–260
    for identifying true or false equations, 268, 271
    for "make a 10" strategy, 163–168
        in adding 9, 217–222
        in adding two numbers, 223–228
    for making true equation, 274
Tens (10)
    adding, 415–420
        in adding two numbers, with ones, 459–470
        in adding two-digit numbers, 477–482
        using mental math, 403–408
        to number, 445–450
        on number line, 421–426, 446, 449, 465–470, 484, 490, 493
    in comparing numbers
        10 more, ten less, 385–390
        11 to 19, 355–360
        within 100, 361–372, 374
    in composing or writing numbers, 311–316
        11 to 19, 305–310
        to 120, 341–346
        counting for, 317–322
        in different ways, 335–340
        quick sketches for, 323–328, 360
        in two-digit number, 329–334
    counting to 120 by, 299–304
    definition of, 306
    in "get to 10" strategy, 261–266, 426
        subtracting 9 in, 255–260

in "make a 10" strategy
    adding 9 in, 217–222
    adding one-digit number to two-digit number in, 471–476
    adding three numbers in, 211–216
    adding two numbers in, 223–228
    finding addends in, 163–168
subtracting, 427–432
    using addition to subtract strategy, 439–444
    using mental math, 409–414
    on number line, 433–438

Tens place, 306, 329–334

Think and Grow, *In every lesson. For example, see:* 4, 66, 128, 188, 244, 294, 356, 404, 460, 504

Think and Grow: Modeling Real Life, *In every lesson. For example, see:* 6, 68, 130, 190, 246, 296, 358, 406, 462, 506

Three-dimensional shapes
    combining to make new shapes, 655–660
    curved surfaces of, 644–648
    describing, 649–654
    edges of, 650–654
    flat surfaces of, 644–654
    sorting, 643–648
    taking apart, 661–666
    vertices of, 649–654

Time, telling
    on analog clock, 583–606
    on digital clock, 601–606
    to half hour, 589–594
    to hour, 583–588
    to hour and half hour, 595–600

Trapezoids
    combining, to make new shapes, 626, 628, 630, 633
    combining shapes to make, 627, 630
    definition of, 620
    describing, 619–624
    equal shares in, identifying, 676, 679
    taking apart shapes containing, 638, 639, 641

Triangles
    combining, to make new shapes, 625–630, 632, 633, 635
    definition of, 620
    describing, 619–624
    equal shares in, identifying, 677
    taking apart shapes containing, 637–642

True equations, finding number making, 273–278

True or false equations
    definition of, 158
    identifying, 157–162, 267–272, 372, 482

Two-digit numbers
    adding one-digit number to, 471–476
    adding using place value, 477–482
    comparing
        1 more, 1 less, 385–390
        10 more, 10 less, 385–390
        11 to 19, 355–360
    comparing, within 100, 361–366
        using number line, 379–384
        using place value, 367–372
        using symbols, 373–378
    understanding place value in, 329–334

Two-dimensional shapes
    closed or open, 614–618
    combining to make new shapes, 625–636
    definition of, 614
    describing, 619–624
    equal shares in
        fourths, 687–692
        halves, 681–686
        identifying, 675–680
    number of sides, 614–624
    number of vertices, 614–624
    sorting, 613–618
    taking apart, 637–642

U

Unequal shares
    definition of, 676
    identifying equal shares *vs.*, 675–680

Unknown(s)
    bigger, compare problems with, 145–150
    smaller, compare problems with, 151–156

Unknown (missing) addends
    add to problems with, 45–50, 127–132
    missing or unknown, making 10, 163–168
    part–part–whole model of, 94, 128–132
    put together problems with, 21–26, 51–56
    ten frame for finding, 100

Unknown change
    add to problems with, 45–50
    take from problems with, 133–138

Unknown start
    add to problems with, 127–132
    take from problems with, 139–144

Vertex (vertices)
    definition of, 614
    of three-dimensional shapes, 649–654
    of two-dimensional shapes
        describing, 619–624
        L-shaped, 615, 616, 619, 622
        sorting by number of, 614–618

Which One Doesn't Belong?, 603, 606

Whole, *See also* Part–part–whole model
    definition of, 16
    equal shares in
        fourths, 687–692
        halves, 681–686
        identifying, 675–680
    put together problems for finding, 15–20
    subtraction equation for finding, 139–144

Word problems, solving
    with addition, 489–494
        within 20, 229–234
    add to, 3–14
    add to, with missing addend, 45–50
    bigger unknown, 145–150
    put together, 15–20
    put together, connected with take apart, 51–56
    put together, missing both addends, 21–26
    with subtraction
        within 20, 279–284
        how many fewer, 39–44
        how many more, 33–38
        smaller unknown, 151–156
        take apart, connected with put together, 51–56
        take from, 27–32

Writing, 549, 552

Writing equations
    addition, 3–8
    subtraction, 28–32

Writing numbers
    11 to 19, 305–310
    to 120, 341–346
    counting by tens and ones for, 317–322
    decade numbers (tens), 311–316
    in different ways, 335–340
    quick sketches for, 323–328, 360
    understanding place value in, 329–334

You Be the Teacher, *Throughout. For example, see:* 79, 115, 231, 275, 301, 411, 479, 505, 597, 677

Zero (0)
    adding, 65–70
    subtracting, 71–76

Reference Sheet

Symbols

+ plus
− minus
= equals
> greater than
< less than

Doubles

1 + 1 = 2	6 + 6 = 12
2 + 2 = 4	7 + 7 = 14
3 + 3 = 6	8 + 8 = 16
4 + 4 = 8	9 + 9 = 18
5 + 5 = 10	10 + 10 = 20

Equal Shares

fourths
quarters

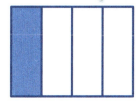
fourth of
quarter of

halves

half of

Time

analog clock

digital clock

An hour is 60 minutes.

A half hour is 30 minutes.

minute hand
hour hand
4 o'clock

half past 4

Two-Dimensional Shapes

 **triangle**	3 straight sides 3 vertices	 **rectangle**	4 straight sides 4 vertices	**square**	4 straight sides 4 vertices
hexagon	6 straight sides 6 vertices	 **trapezoid**	4 straight sides 4 vertices	 **rhombus**	4 straight sides 4 vertices

Three-Dimensional Shapes

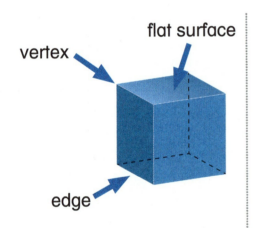

vertex, flat surface, edge

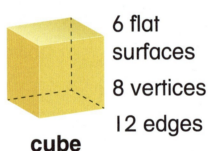 **cube** — 6 flat surfaces, 8 vertices, 12 edges

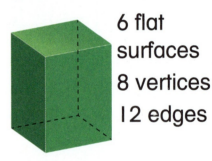 **rectangular prism** — 6 flat surfaces, 8 vertices, 12 edges

 **cone** — 1 flat surface, 1 vertex, 0 edges

 **cylinder** — 2 flat surfaces, 0 vertices, 0 edges

 **sphere** — 0 flat surfaces, 0 vertices, 0 edges

© Big Ideas Learning, LLC

Credits

Chapter 1
1 Rike_/iStock/Getty Images Plus

Chapter 2
63 Liliboas/E+/Getty Images; **80** Aratehortua/Shutterstock.com

Chapter 3
125 Nastco/iStock/Getty Images Plus, taratata/iStock/Getty Images Plus

Chapter 4
185 macrovector/iStock/Getty Images Plus

Chapter 5
241 DiyanaDimitrova/iStock/Getty Images Plus

Chapter 6
291 shutter_m/iStock/Getty Images Plus

Chapter 7
353 keita/iStock/Getty Images Plus

Chapter 8
401 PaulMichaelHughes/iStock/Getty Images Plus

Chapter 9
457 FatCamera/E+/Getty Images

Chapter 10
501 muchomor/iStock/Getty Images Plus

Chapter 11
539 PeopleImages/iStock/Getty Images Plus

Chapter 12
581 kali9/iStock/Getty Images Plus

Chapter 13
611 Jon (https://commons.wikimedia.org/wiki/File:Ultimate_Sand_Castle.jpg), „Ultimate Sand Castle", https://creativecommons.org/licenses/by/2.0/legalcode

Chapter 14
673 mediaphotos/iStock/Getty Images Plus

Cartoon Illustrations: MoreFrames Animation
Design Elements: oksanika/Shutterstock.com; icolourful/Shutterstock.com; Valdis Torms